PUNISHMENT

PATTERSON SMITH REPRINT SERIES IN
CRIMINOLOGY, LAW ENFORCEMENT, AND SOCIAL PROBLEMS

A listing of publications in the SERIES *will be found at rear of volume*

PUBLICATION No. 147: PATTERSON SMITH REPRINT SERIES IN CRIMINOLOGY, LAW ENFORCEMENT, AND SOCIAL PROBLEMS

PUNISHMENT

ITS ORIGIN, PURPOSE AND PSYCHOLOGY

BY

HANS VON HENTIG

REPRINTED WITH THE ADDITION OF
A NEW PREFACE BY THE AUTHOR
AND AN INDEX

MONTCLAIR, NEW JERSEY
PATTERSON SMITH
1973

First published 1937 by William Hodge & Company Ltd.
Reprinted 1973, with permission, by
Patterson Smith Publishing Corporation
Montclair, New Jersey 07042
New material copyright © 1973 by
Patterson Smith Publishing Corporation

Library of Congress Cataloging in Publication Data

Hentig, Hans von, 1887–
    Punishment.
    (Patterson Smith reprint series in criminology, law
enforcement, and social problems. Publication no. 147)
    Reprint of the 1937 ed. with a new author's
preface and an index.
    Translation of Die Strafe.
    1. Punishment. I. Title.

HV8667.H42 1973   364.6   74-172566
            ISBN 0-87585-147-9

PREFACE TO THE REPRINT EDITION

IN the forty years since this book was first published, it seems that punishment—the oldest of all institutions governing human society—has been more and more beset by problems. The rule of law has yielded to the personal element which vacillates capriciously from one opinion to another. Dictatorship and brutal ruthlessness give way to weak permissiveness. Punishment and society itself come under indictment as we await a return to normality.

Thus we see international skyjackers and revolutionary groups holding captives for ransom and inflicting "people's justice" according to their own rules. These groups have taken punishment out of the hands of the state, applying their own laws and sanctions when society does not bend to their will. In their quest to set the world aright, their own security requires them to resort to means of execution which are scarcely different from murder.

Considered purely as a means of safeguarding human society, a system of punishment requires powerful motivating forces behind its actuation, its regulation, and its rational administration. Here we are faced with an abundance of human problems erratically affecting the function and the effectiveness of the instrument of punishment, which can become refined or coarsened as changes take place in our spiritual development. Human progress—still more, human decline—is reflected in our need to punish and in our skill in carrying it out.

Early lawgivers, such as Moses, Numa, Solon, and Lycurgus, were pedagogues to their peoples. Lycurgus would have nothing of written laws, speaking of the constraint of the written word. Mindful of the changeableness of all forms

v

of life, he would leave the door open for modifications and reforms. Solon also governed with flexibility and moderation, although his reforms did not survive. Numa and Moses responded to divine commands; if their laws proved rigid and inflexible, this was due to the absolute nature of heavenly edicts.

Modern legislatures are exposed to the opposite danger. They frequently give in to outbreaks of sentimentality, allowing themselves to be led astray by this or that event which moves them deeply and overpowers their better judgment. In recent times the temptation to abolish burdensome laws has become stronger and stronger during periods of crisis, as a cheap means of courting popularity. This legislative complaisance takes the guise of progress and understanding, especially in the case of much-debated moral transgressions, which multiply in times of stress or shed their veil of secrecy. Offenses such as abortion, whose criminality was never before in doubt, share this fate. Similarly the death penalty comes and goes with the tides of violence and contempt for others' lives, ever a gauge of our rising and falling feelings of fear.

In our courts of law, wherein the death penalty confers life-giving power, it is the judge, I feel, who is the leading figure. Criminal procedure in all countries has given the judge authority to set aside the legally prescribed punishment with a stroke of the pen. According to the German Code of Criminal Procedure,

> Violations of the law will not be prosecuted when the guilt of the perpetrator is trifling and the consequences of the deed are insignificant, unless it is in the public interest to reach a judicial decision.
>
> If in a misdemeanor the guilt of the perpetrator is trifling and the consequences insignificant, the public prosecutor may, with the concurrence of the district judge, decide against public prosecution.

In the United States the acceptance by the court of a plea

of "guilty to a reduced charge" bestows upon the judge a partial right of pardon. From this encroachment on the legally prescribed code of punishment the judge derives additional power. There are further ways in which the penal code is weakened. In securing acquittal, the charm of the accused often plays a part as well as objective considerations. And few will doubt the power of first-class defense attorneys to obtain reduced sentences for their clients—especially in murder cases and in American courts. These defense counsels, and many judges and legal experts, are supported by a morally crippled public. Criminal instincts that should be extirpated in their first stages, when they are still weak and hesitant, are instead nourished by the broad sections of the community whose permissive, inwardly torn mentalities prevent them from pronouncing a firm, decisive "No!" Society and the institution of punishment are clearly in the throes of transition during present times, when throughout the world there seems to be an almost pathological reluctance to make a rational response to assault and wrongdoing.

HANS VON HENTIG.

BAD TÖLZ, BAVARIA
October 1972

PREFACE TO THE ENGLISH EDITION, 1937

THIS book and its appearance need an explanation. My design is to put a few facts and suggestions about criminal punishment before the English public. In order to impress the mind of reasoning people (they, not the learned scholars, make good and bad laws) it was necessary to be as clear and simple as possible. For this purpose I have omitted the numerous footnotes of the German edition. The specialist who wishes to refer to the sources employed will find these in the German and Danish editions and in the Italian or Spanish translations, now in preparation.

The chapter " Sterilization and Castration " has been rewritten for this edition.

HANS VON HENTIG.

NEW HAVEN (CONN.),
   U.S.A.

CONTENTS

CONTENTS

CHAPTER I

THE SCOPE AND LIMITS OF PUNISHMENT

Flight from a destructive stimulus is one of the most decisive reactions of living matter, in so far as it has developed stimulus-conveying organs and mechanisms of movement. In sudden withdrawal from the destructive sphere, the sensory touch of many animals offers a preliminary and abbreviated act of flight. The far-reaching senses of smell, hearing, and sight apprehended the threatening stimulus, while it is still in the neighbourhood of the body, thus allowing of a timely parrying movement. Again, there are deposited in the brain countless condensed experiences of situations which threaten life; thus the conception of danger sets the adequate reaction in motion long before its actual approach. This is the strongest tendency of all life, and with it the social contrivance of punishment reckons. Punishment is not confined to law, although there it finds its harshest form and most energetic expression; its application enters into every human relationship, indeed into every relationship to which the imagination gives human shape: religion, education, politics, and even aimless games all incorporate its principles.

Punishment means the establishment of artificial danger. Punishment is organized hurt, an impairment of life organized in the form of laws, which society consciously uses to train humanity to avoid certain possible courses of action potentially injurious or hostile to itself. Punishment is imitation of precedents which in real life

1

are hourly repeated: here lurks the injurious agent, and there, guarded by man's living senses, wait the motor functions, and over both mechanisms is their great co-ordinator, the Brain. With sound co-operation the stimulus which cannot be overcome or surmounted will be avoided, circumvented, or rendered harmless by flight.

Thus a condition of the efficacy of punishment is a sane impulsiveness, which is sensible of the harm as pain, which has stored it in its reservoir of conceptions as pain, and which mechanically transforms the experience or idea of pain into repulsion. Another condition is a state of life so constituted that the senses' conception of the artificially engendered pain, with its restraining action and the feelings' appreciation of it and their united reflex on the mechanical apparatus, do not meet with interference in the brain itself. Strong, positively accentuated emotions and tendencies can withstand the change into inhibitions by reason of their greater intensity. But should artificially erected sensation of impending damage come into conflict with innate sensation of attraction, then the action develops now on this, now on that, side, according to its affinity to this or that agent. Punishment can only be tuned to the moral pitch of the average man in an average position of life. It must fail whenever these assumed conditions are in any way altered. Far from being a difficult problem, punishment would be a mere arithmetical exercise if sensitiveness were always normal and healthy. We know, however, that man's instinct of self-preservation (the unit with which punishment reckons and works) can be disordered, peaky, perverted, or gravely ill. There are phases in life when one would call it ill, such as when ultra-individual aims demand its attenuation while

2

it is leading its own life with undiminished vigour. Self-preservation is here clearly only a subordinate function of the preservation of the species and in the psyche of man there are arranged mechanisms to allow of the periodical diminution of this powerful instinct. The development of the sphere of moral feelings, which would be physiologically suspended in the air without organic base, is perhaps only a kind of undulatory phase which, becoming fixed and through selection and exercise deeper and deeper rooted, has, in addition to the care of the young, taken other objects, its fellow-beings, under its care and protection. If the self-preservation instinct is lulled at such periods, then the threat to life contained in punishment is of no avail. Fear of punishment, as well as experience of punishment, dashes against the harder surface of a psychically exceptional position and, far from fulfilling their purpose, only blunt themselves.

The history of civilization further teaches us that there are periods in which, for reasons unknown, man's instinct of self-preservation as a universal phenomenon is reduced and gives place to an instinctive tendency towards destruction and even self-destruction. These periods have a certain resemblance to the crisis of puberty in youth, except that this critical reversal extends to all ages. At such times we see the younger generations supplanting the older in leadership; the entire political, social, and cultural life takes on the lively and varied tints of the pubescent psyche in which the darker shades of depressive fits and senseless self-sacrifice are not absent. If youth seizes power and begins to experiment in politics, then, vaguely distrustful of its own impulsive fearlessness and avidity for danger, it intensifies the harshness of the threats of the penal code. But here, too, the psychical armour retains its superiority in the contest with the percussive force of the pain or threat of punishment.

Besides these periodical fluctuations the self-preservation instinct of individuals can be so weakened or crippled that its inversion becomes a source of pleasure. Chronic forms of mental depression show the sunken level of the life tension. The pessimist's conclusion of life's futility is only an outward projection of his own tiredness of life. A more serious symptom of a morbid failure of the self-preservation instinct is the refusal of food; still more serious is ' conscientious objection ' in the field of sexual intercourse. These troubles are present in the most varied mental disorders and it is not always easy to distinguish whether the vital force is primarily affected, or superimposed delusions, or a conscious suicidal tendency play a secondary part.

Like the loss of pleasure in food and sexual intercourse, the surrender to harmful poisons producing a transitory pleasurable effect can be diagnosed as a disorder of the self-preservation instinct. It is true that drunkenness ' brought about by one's own fault ' is mentioned in jurisprudence and the legislature, yet we know that these things do not belong only to the sphere of ' free-will.' Many people enjoy these poisons without getting drunk; they are able to stop when they wish, their actions having little or no connexion with the poisons, which are quickly washed out of the body. It is, however, evident that in others the tendency to misuse these poisons is latent; in them a distinct avoidance of the more vivid pleasureable excitements is inherent, as also is distinct incontinence, and especially the inclination towards a progressive taking of poisons. Such a tendency and development betray the weak foundations of the self-

4

preservation instinct. With this type of person punishment is useless, because the conditions of its efficacy are inadequate.

Self-injury and self-mutilation, in cases of a considerable diminution of the normal sensitivity to pain, also betray a deficient tendency to flee from the destructive stimulus. Here is such a reversal of conditions that with it a continuance of life is in the long run irreconcilable. One must not look for self-injury in its grossest forms. What we call progress, by which I do not mean technical improvements, but a finer expansion of those conceptions which govern the communal life of man, has been almost entirely brought about by traumatophiles. These men did not overlook the difficulties they raised for themselves, but the deadly resistance of a world infinitely stronger than they drew them on, as the magnetic mountain draws the ship in the fable. In their mania for wounds they disregarded the State's threats of punishment, and, as if fulfilling an ardent desire, stabbed themselves with the weapons with which the law sought to prevent their further teaching or progress. No wonder that punishment, their reward, had no power over these men.

A clearer and simpler expression of a diseased self-preservation instinct is suicide, and if one subtracts the disorders so far described, the number of suicides is alone sufficient to establish the wide prevalence of the instinct of self-destruction. At the same time we must not forget that in addition to successful suicides there are the unsuccessful attempts; and that hidden among fatal accidents there is a large number of undiscovered or unadmitted suicides. In the numerous accidents which statistics show to be the fault of the victim or injured, one is justified in presuming the presence of that lesser

5

form of suicidal tendency which lies in chronic gross carelessness and which is often noticeable in the passionate quest of dangerous situations (mountaineering, parachute-jumping, &c.). The untameable and ever-renewed pugnacity of youth has, because it contains a strong element of unselfishness, been made to serve the purposes of the State for as long as man has been organized into groups. Here, of course, it is only a case of gambling with the life of the youth for the life of the State, of purchasing a gain of life with a sacrifice of life. Only now has the destructive effect of modern mechanical warfare begun to shake the accuracy of this equation, because the tremendous loss of life can no longer be made good by the material gain.

The disorders of self-preservation and the weaknesses of the preservation of the species are in many ways correlated. From the abatement of sexual lust, and from its transference to objects unserviceable for propagation, the rungs of the ladder lead to the worst forms of masochism, in which the natural avoidance of pain has completely disappeared and the reception of pain becomes an aphrodisiac. Here, indeed, are some degenerate relations to that period of struggle and wounds, of fighting for the sexual partner, in which the sense of pain must be reduced. In a case of well-marked masochism the sense of pain, the warning of biological damage, is completely lost and the point is reached at which a purely destructive action is turned into sexual attraction. One may expect that such degenerates will not avoid punishment, but may even seek it, especially as the application of the pleasurably exciting drug ' Punishment ' is taken up by the State, at its expense and with all its majesty.

Since corporal punishment has practically disappeared in Europe and the death penalty has become more and more rare, the form of penal sanctions has altered. Physical interference with the criminal which threatens his life or health is not openly adopted. Deprivation of freedom, which is the main resort nowadays, is so managed that evident damage to health can be repaired by medical attention. The effect of punishment is more and more concentrated upon the mental sphere or upon such physical harms as from their nature are possible to foresee, but which are lingering and not immediately perceptible to the untrained eye. This change in turn produces a curtailment of susceptibility to punishment.

A later development of the self-preservation instinct is possessiveness. The origins of possessiveness were the retention and defence of prey or the food store and the acquisition of a mate; and even to-day one can observe how an animal will appropriate a particular hunting area to its exclusive use for hunting and for subduing its mate. In man generally possessiveness is very highly developed, but cases of a weakened possessiveness, which can assume a self-threatening form, especially in northern climes where it is difficult to maintain life without making some provision for the future, are not uncommon.

While it is chiefly the pre-senile and senile ages that are affected by a morbid exaggeration of the need of possessions (it is also, however, found fairly frequently in women and children), weakening of possessiveness is most apt to occur during puberty and adolescence, when, indeed, it is the normal condition. Real lovers, for example, are true spendthrifts, and there can be no better warning for a girl than stinginess in her professed admirer. On the other hand, many poisons, such as alcohol, awaken the wastrel in a man, and when drinkers sing and fraternize, when they extol wine, woman, and song, then one must not forget their enthusiasm for

7

community of possessions. The spendthrift impulse also occurs in manic phases and general paralysis, though here the extravagance seems to be conditioned rather by the subject's insane delusions of fabulous riches. Indifference to property is sometimes also the result of a depressive mental disorder or of the decay of personality arising from endogenous psychosis. There are few lawyers who have not had experience of some such case. A man, after making unaccountably lavish gifts, develops a manifest melancholia and his committee in lunacy has to institute proceedings to set aside his dispositions.

Women seem to have stronger possessiveness than men. This is presumably merely a question of derivated instinct, the instinct that is normally expressed in the protection and care of the young. Should this remain biologically unused, it can, as it were, make itself independent, and will then be used for purely selfish ends. Extreme possessiveness is characteristic of many Lesbian women, as well as elderly childless spinsters. Here, in the woman who is growing old, the accumulation of possessions clearly takes the place of the assistance usually rendered by the family group. The frequency of murder with the motive of robbery in this class of humanity can be traced back to the covetousness of such women and the isolation consequent on their disposition.

Where degenerate tendencies or a psychical callousness, on which the psychiatrist's needle or more drastic artificial hurts have no lasting reaction, lead to ineffectiveness of imprisonment, which takes desire for freedom and need for locomotion for granted, it is evident that indifference to or hate of possessions must destroy the power of fines as a punishment, the latter being based on the normal characteristic of the desire for money and possessions. In such cases the normal method of punishment must fail, however effective, objectively regarded, it might be in itself, because various steps in the psychological equation are wrong, and the artificially planned sequence of cause and effect, instead of meshing, meets with gaps in its continuity, and therefore runs without load.

In all the cases we have so far touched upon, the subject can be assumed to be aware of the nature of punishment as a vital damage, even if the damage be one to which he is indifferent. But in many mental disorders, such as the confusional condition of epileptics, any threat of punishment is futile, because the higher mental life is extinguished and with it the apprehension of any inhibitive conceptions. The subject may also in his madness imagine a situation or crisis that calls for self-defence, and in this case his actions will be governed, not by the menacing punishment for killing, but by his imagined justification of self-defence.

Nearer to the normal mentality are those crimes where punishment is ineffective because the perpetrator has resolved upon suicide—that is to say, his plans for flight have a perfectly sound foundation. Here I am thinking chiefly of what may be called the ' follow-your-victim ' murder, in which a lover kills his sweetheart or a father his wife, daughter, or family, and then turns his hand against himself. Often the murder uses up the available store of inner tension, so that none is left for the suicide. Sometimes, as in the so-called ' suicide pacts,' where a man and a woman resolve to kill themselves by gas poisoning, the man survives because he is the stronger. Such acts can only be explained on the supposition that the perpetrator fully believed that by his decision to die, he had eliminated all possibility of punishment, even

9

though at the last moment he did not carry out his object or was saved contrary to his intention.

Such a person, like the political assassin who is set upon dying, is obviously beyond the range of penal sanctions, because punishment presupposes the fear of suffering, and so the will to live. The will to suffer and even more the will not to live, demonstrate that penal sanctions like everything else have definite limits; and it is proper that the State should know what these limits are in order that it may devise complementary methods for the prevention of crime.

So far we have proceeded on the assumption that punishment, objectively regarded, is truly a restriction of life, though its painful quality in this respect is not felt by certain degenerate forms of man's psychical mechanism. If the normal relation between self-interest and a threatening external stimulus is deranged, so, too, is the normal defensive reaction, which is either absent or perverted to positive appetition.

Nevertheless, it is possible for the instinct of self-preservation to be undamaged in essentials and yet for punishment to be ineffective. The threat of punishment throws a motive into an arena in which new gladiators are continually being matched. An evil is brought into view, which, with a normal distribution of psychical balance, would drive impulse from the field. But this incentive is not a fixed, but an extremely variable quantity, which may be reduced or magnified according to the individual's disposition. The extent of variation far exceeds that of the discretion which a judge is allowed in passing sentence.

Just as there are narcotic substances that ease bodily pain, so there are psychical narcotics derived from ideas and certain emotional states. The fear of pain, upon

10

which punishment reckons, can be dulled or annulled by stronger notions. Note, however, that these over-ruling ideas are not necessarily morbid; on the contrary, one of the most vital of the State's measures of self-assertion is based on the possibility of such a com-mutation of motive. It would be absurd to expect a man to lead a platoon into action under a heavy bombard-ment, were it not possible to flood out his natural fear of death with streams of altruistic feeling from a suddenly opened sluice. Another example is the early Christians' contempt for death, where the belief in future bliss overcame the universal fear of destruction and extinction—a psychic revolution which turned the law's punishment into a passionately desired reward and paralysed its social function once and for all.

The cultural worth of other narcotic ideas is disputed. But it is certain that, in the unselfish initial stages of many great revolutionary movements, there was deep social consciousness. It is just the revolutionary's con-tempt for death which, compared with the other side's normal capacity for fear of it, is his weapon of victory. It is from his knowledge of his own changed mentality, from a projection of fearlessness rather than from fits of fright, that the real revolutionary gets his preference for the radical method of ' cleaning up '—the death penalty—which, to be sure, has at all times been the most unsafe of safety methods, because these dead assuredly return.

Presented in group or mass formation, strong political, religious, or social ideas may set up an opposition to law and order. This, of course, is often merely the first step to ascendancy and indemnity; the minority may become, not the majority, but the ruler. But even where there is no such hope, it is always easier to

11

show a bold front to authority in the company of others, however few they may be. On the other hand, adherence to a minority group is not necessarily the result of genuine conviction. It may be merely imitative, the result of suggestion, without any intellectual or motional foundation; and in such a case the threat of punishment is often effective.

Much deeper are the roots of the conflict where the individual, actuated by a motive that is supposedly if not actually higher, sets himself in opposition to the dictates of the law. Often the law makes allowance for this dilemma as in the case of the refusal of a fiancé or relation to give evidence against an accused person (§ 52, Germ. S.T.P.O.), or of the shielding of a culprit by relations (§ 257, 2 S.T.P.O.), but many cases of conflict between ' behaviour motive ' (*e.g.*, friendship) and ' threat motive ' are not recognized by the law. We have already spoken about what may be called ' extended suicide,' *i.e.*, when the suicide is preceded by the murder of one or more loved ones. Pity and anxiety for those who would be left behind very often guide the hand of the suicide. The taking of the family to the grave with one is an act of providing for them.* The perpetrator

---

* Christian Holzwart, who on 29th December, 1845, murdered his wife and five children and gravely injured himself, gave the following answer to the examining magistrate: " Yes, I am guilty," he said quietly and firmly. " It is my fault, but it is not the work of a momentary sudden idea. For years I have had the opportunity to observe how I and my family are under an unlucky star; my circumstances became worse and worse and I became convinced that we would be reduced to beggary. This idea accompanied me as I raised my hand to kill my wife and children. No other reason than love of my family would ever have induced me to carry out such a difficult deed. Love gave me the strength to remove them all from the world, who in my judgment would soon be helpless and humiliated. They did not suffer. Unconsciously and gladly they saw without pain the approach of the last minutes of their existence. I began with my wife and ended with my youngest daughter. . . . I put off doing it from one day to another—and I was willing to

12

having himself decided to die, does not fear interference from the law. Pity, however, plays no mean rôle in other punishable actions, such as perjury, aiding and abetting prison-breaking, obstruction of officials in the execution of their duties, and other offences; if even here a sudden passion comes into play, so (at the decisive moment at least) punishment will be ethically dethroned and deprived of power. Small social groups, such as the village, the family, lovers, have as the chief element of their social function a narrow, practically unconditional cohesion, off whose smooth surface the threat of punishment glides almost as a matter of course. The family, the friend, the sweetheart, or the ring of the same village or the same race will defy every threat of punishment and enter the lists on behalf of an accused person, and commit perjury without scruple.

Punishment may also fail for other reasons. It not only presupposes a sound instinct of self-preservation, but must also neutralize any idea of criminal success by instilling counter-ideas. The counter-idea, however, can only be effective if either it is given a stronger accent in the consciousness or has at least the same objective value as the prohibited gratification. To take a good example, German law allows the normally constituted person a wide choice of ways in which to get rid of sexual stress, and hence without being Utopian

---

go out of the world alone, but my love for my family revolted against this. I would be all right after the terrible struggle, but they? Oh, I saw them the victims of poverty, vileness, and depravity! No, together out of the world—together into peace . . . ! " Holzwart was condemned to death. Then the revolution of 1848 broke out and he was pardoned on 18th April, 1849, and the sentence commuted to penal servitude for life. On Sunday, 20th January, 1850, Holzwart threw himself from the topmost gallery into the prison hall and lay there with a split skull and shattered limbs.—" Der Neue Pitaval," 25 Teil, Dritte Folge, Erster Teil, Leipzig, 1858, pp. 70-143.

in its psychology, can forbid a large number of sexual actions, such as indecent behaviour to children, rape, and seduction. No doubt that the fear of punishment is in very many cases an effective deterrent. On the other hand, in the case of sexual degenerates the normally wide scope of sexual action is narrowed down to a single point, being some form of perversion which comes into conflict with the law. If the true homosexual or exhibitionist compares his only method of relief, which is extraordinarily attractive because it is the only one, with the small evil of the punishment, then the punishment easily loses its motivating power. We know, indeed, from experience that even a far more severe punishment would hardly be adequate against this highly intractable psychic state.

There is yet another difficulty. A criminal act (*e.g.*, theft, murder, rape) is directed towards an immediate satisfaction—immediacy is of its essence—whereas punishment is remote. As compared with crime's effect, punishment is a slow and complicated process. First, the crime must be discovered, then we have to trace the criminal, catch him, and finally convict him. Every one of these steps is beset by obstacles. Here lies, in practice, the chief problem of punishment. How can uncertain punishment compete successfully in the criminal's mind with certain satisfaction? The law's only answer hitherto has been to increase the severity of its punishments instead of perfecting the machinery of detection and proof; and little or no consideration has been given to the fact that the moron, the youth greedy for adventure and the reckless gambler will always take a rosy view of the chance of ' getting away with it,' and therefore fear punishment just about as much as the atheist fears Hell.

SCOPE AND LIMITS OF PUNISHMENT

In more credulous and primitive times the difficulties were less. Objectively the situation was the same, but in the mind of the criminal there was the certainty, or at least the unresolved fear, that the gods would betray the guilty one and would demonstrate the truth by a miracle or, at any rate, through the mouth of initiated priests. So, from the culprit's point of view, the certainty of discovery was much greater than to-day, in spite of all our apparatus of wireless, finger-prints, and *portrait parlé*. We do not need to go back to classical or Germanic antiquity for examples. Shortly before the war the Bergdama in German South-west Africa, made use of the witch doctors to ascertain an unknown evil-doer. True, this magic ritual was effectively aided by a technique of tracking which is particularly highly developed in these tribes. In Papua and Melanesia, too, the detective procedure is, presumably to this day, provided by the oracle. As long as these people believe that their misdeeds can be brought to light through the immediate intervention of the gods (just as the Indians of the Veda era, the Greeks, the Romans, and the Germans knew the judgment of the gods) the certainty of punishment is to a high degree guaranteed, and punishment can successfully compete with the satisfaction to be gained from the criminal act.

All these objections concern the psychological limitations of punishment. There are, however, other limitations of a sociological character. Punishment carries with it social degradation, which has motivating force as a curtailment of existence. This assumes, of course, that the culprit has hitherto enjoyed a tolerable position in life—more tolerable, that is, than imprisonment. But unfortunately the assumption is not always justified. There is such a thing as acute economic distress. We

15

have seen how mass unemployment can plunge millions into hunger and privation, through no fault of their own. In such a case the healthy self-preservation instinct can but choose the lesser evil—that is, punishment plus food, clothing and warmth. Where life is harder than the punishment of man, law and order stands at the limit of its power.

CHAPTER II

THE EVOLUTION OF PUNISHMENT

1. EXPULSION

In the course of centuries Punishment has, as it were, moved in a circle. The idea of doing some deliberate harm to another was no part of its original character. It was simply a defensive reaction, and one of the most effective methods of self-defence is to kill your enemy. The time came when the slackening of the tension of excited passion achieved a value of its own, and, to justify itself, devised all sorts of disinterested and noble-hearted theories. To-day we are approaching the point at which reconstructed punishment resumes its purely defensive character.

Society's simplest form of self-defence is outlawry. In primitive social conditions the individual's greatest good is his share in a community of peace and law. Inside the community is life; outside the social group lies danger, the superior forces of nature, of human and animal enemies, so that, in addition to the painful frustration of the animal herd instinct, which is especially strong in primitive peoples, exclusion from the group implies helplessness and destruction as well. Whereas it is necessary to-day to set up an artificial danger in the shape of Punishment, in those days the mere withdrawal of the common support sufficed to plunge the criminal into extreme bodily danger. There no longer existed a helping order whose united forces counterbalanced, to a certain extent, the fury of nature and the attacks of ravening animals or human enemies. The criminal was, it is true, still alive, but very near destruction, and, with the ties of kindred, marriage, and blood-friendship severed, deprived of house and land, the dark forest became his home and his grave.

The outlawry of olden days was thus a method of killing the outlaw without raising a hand against him. The defensive circle of the tribe opened and thrust him out to the death which lay in wait for the solitary man, even when he was not followed into the forest and killed. One can, however, only expel from an advantageous situation, from security into danger, from the protection of the community into the defencelessness of isolation.

As the forest was cleared and the world grew more habitable and the little societies became less isolated, outlawry gradually lost its chief terrors. Abandonment to nature no longer meant certain death. The outlaw could seek admission to another community without being repulsed as a matter of course. Nevertheless, even in the Middle Ages, expulsion from one's city could be a terrible and effective punishment, especially when it was coupled with distinctive mutilations and its victim was of humble condition and without means. His life was spared in his home town only that he might end it on the gallows of the next. Banishment had the apparent advantage of cheapness: you got rid of your criminals by passing them on to the next town. But as the next town returned the compliment by passing its criminals on to you, not much was gained. Such a system of ' general post ' was obviously of no use to the body politic at large. Indeed, it was worse than useless; for the outcast was *ipso facto* a pauper, and, as mental defectives were also dealt with by banishment,

18

these forced exchanges only aggravated the original mischief.

Even modern civilized societies use outlawry, though in the modified form of a social ostracism as distinguished from a legal penalty. It often happens that a family wants to cut itself off from the son who has been in prison; or a father may say, " This woman is no longer my daughter.'' As in the outlawry of olden days, the delinquent is driven out from a defensive circle and ' thrown to the wolves,' which in this case are the destructive forces of our complicated civilization. Similarly, any association which gives its members a privileged position (*e.g.*, a club, a students' corps or fraternity, or a ruling party as in Russia, Germany, Italy, &c.) has the power to punish by expulsion. The Church, again, has its own species of outlawry—excommunication, which in former times could bend, if not break, even princes and emperors. But occasionally the converse of outlawry occurs. An offender may happen to be indispensable to the community, and to expel him would be cutting off one's nose to spite one's face. In such a case the only way to punish him is by strict confinement within the city walls. Thus the artist and forger, Veit Stoss, was first branded, but as his banishment would have deprived Nürnberg of a world-famous woodcarver—that is to say, would have been against the public interest—he was as a punishment *detained* in the city ' for ever '; which sentence lasted until the Emperor Maximilian signed his pardon.

Often it was only in order to protect the offender from the vengeance of his enemies, and to put a stop to bloodshed that he was driven from the city bounds. In this way the contending parties were separated for good—a procedure which compares favourably with

19

our modern practice of giving the disturber of the peace a short and futile term of imprisonment from which he emerges to renew the strife. A similar idea was at the bottom of the Athenian ostracism—exclusion from the country was simultaneously seclusion and a diversion of the chronic sources of conflict. It was enough for social peace if the party, who was for the time being the weaker, gave way.

2. REVENGE

The development of legal punishment to its present state has been a slow process, arrested at times, at times even retrograde. Indeed, the general idea of punishment in practice has altered only in so far as the persons of the injured party and he who inflicts the punishment (or in the case of a fine, he who receives it) have been separated; and any progress that has been made towards a systematic treatment of the criminal problem is the result of this differentiation, which makes one who has not been wronged decide on the State's reaction. The moment the injured party takes the law into his own hands, we slip back, so to speak, thousands of years, and although nowadays such a lapse may not involve a blood feud, that is only because family ties have not their ancient strictness. The shadows of the past may have faded before the light of our workaday world, but they still lurk and have power in the secret recesses of our emotions. Hence it is easy for us to err in our treatment of the criminal; for, whether from a vague sense of danger or from putting ourselves too thoroughly in the place of the injured party, we are apt to see ourselves as injured parties, from which it follows that the only effective defence and ' just ' punishment is the destruction of the aggressor.

20

EVOLUTION OF PUNISHMENT

Revenge is the origin of all legal policy and administration of justice. In the form of the blood feud it is the supplementary—and at the same time anticipatory—self-defence of the family group, which has been weakened by the killing or wounding of one of its members. As the aggression is regarded, not as a crime against the individual, but as an attack on the tribe, the ensuing blood feud is a racial affair. The reprisals are directed against the aggressor's whole race, its present and future operative strength. The contending parties are not individuals, human atoms without any social worth, but small unitary groups which can live only as such. They are, as a matter of course, assumed to be jointly and severally responsible for the actions of their individual members, and they accept this responsibility without demur. The group or tribe feels the death of the individual as a loss of power in the struggle for existence, and ruthlessly takes action against the competing group to equalize the loss.

The blood feud is primarily a duty rather than a right, though in the defensive emotions right and duty are barely distinguishable. Self-defence and the private danger it occasions, it may be said, by custom and by religious sanctions, have created a single moral obligation which binds all equally. Strictly speaking, only serious infringements of the law are subjects of vengeance. Killing as the cause of a blood feud carries us back to an older stratum of conceptions, to which the later rational conception of self-defence is as foreign as the idea of ' honour or posthumous fame ' of the dead as Wilda expressed it many years ago. This coercive form of vengeance, the true blood feud, was originally a manifestation of the cult of the soul; souls were not yet, as later, elevated to peace, or dispatched to some mythical place of reunion. They were present among the living, sometimes benevolent, sometimes angrily prowling about with evil intent, especially in the case of those whose thread of life had been rudely, untimely, and forcibly broken. As we know from the vampire belief, the sacrifice of the enemy propitiates the soul which craves for the life forces that inhabit the blood. By slaying the murderer the avenger averts a danger more serious than the risk of pressing and fighting a living enemy. On the other hand, we often find vengeance extended to bodily injuries and sexual aggression, and among one or two peoples it has so far degenerated from its original idea as to be employed against quite trivial wrongs.

As a general rule, the duty of the blood feud falls upon the nearest male relation of the victim. The blood feud is not always directed against the actual aggressor, but often against the head of the family or other authoritative male relation. According to Islamic law, blood feud is permitted against the active participant, but not against the accessories before or after the crime. Children, women and old men are sometimes exempt, but this rule does not hold good everywhere.

The blood feud originally was not, or was very little, concerned with guilt. Thus, in the formal declaration of protection made by the judge to the executioner in the Middle Ages, we may have the remains of an idea that the execution might justify a blood feud. But no such notion ever attached to killing in battle.

The idea among primitive peoples that an attempted action carried with it the same responsibility as the same action successfully completed, thus leading to a blood feud, generally lost prevalence. Its development can be particularly well traced in the Mosaic law. Moses ordained the blood feud for ' murder,' but one can hardly agree with Michaelis when he makes a distinction between murder and manslaughter, supposing for murder death, and for manslaughter compulsory residence in a city of refuge till the death of the high priest, which was the occasion of a kind of moral general amnesty. A killing which resulted in a blood feud was in Mosaic law dependent on three conditions. The first was the psychological motive, the deed being done from enmity, hatred or bloodthirstiness. Then came an aggravating mode of action, artifice or ambush. Finally, a presumption of guilt could arise from the instrument used or the manner of perpetration. Thus it is murder when an iron or wooden instrument or the fist is used, when the man is thrown down or made to fall. " The avenger shall kill the murderer when he comes across him."

Evidently, then, many acts that would be manslaughter according to modern legal conceptions fall within the Mosaic conception of murder and would give rise to a blood feud. It was the duty of the victim's nearest relation to kill the murderer, wherever he might find him, except in holy places. Michaelis has proposed ' the stained with blood ' as a translation for ' goel,' the Hebrew word for avenger. The victim's nearest relation was treated as if infected, until he had washed away the infection by exacting vengeance. According to Michaelis, even the Arabs regarded a victim's relation as contaminated until he had restored his honour by exacting vengeance. He who failed to avenge the death of a relation was as much disgraced as a German officer who declines a duel.

What Michaelis, on the other hand, calls manslaughter, would to-day be called killing by negligence,

23

sometimes even death by misadventure—even if the word ' unintentionally ' was not specifically mentioned, or the lack of motive accentuated, or where it was a question of pure chance.* The blood feud was too much a categorical imperative of the ancient cult of the dead as well as of excited passions for it to be countered by social or religious regulations. The effect of Moses' wise foresight in establishing havens was not only to defend the slayer from the avenger, but also to protect the avenger from precipitation and excess. According to tradition, there were at first three cities in which the fugitive was inviolable, and after the conquest of West Jordania three more were set up.

To adopt the course of flight was to exile oneself—self-banishment, just as in Roman law. Its severity lay in the fact that, among a nation of peasants, the exile was separated from the soil which nourished him and could not go more than 1000 ells outside the walls of the little city of refuge without endangering his life.

The refuge city offered only a qualified protection lasting until the community had passed judgment on the deed. Should the fugitive be found guilty of killing with hostile intent, or with a murderous weapon, then he had to be delivered up to the avenger. It had thus already developed beyond the rough form of the right of asylum which we find even to-day in Togoland (surrender by the fetish priests against payment of one sheep and 24,000 cowries or one year's service as the fetish priests' slave). In the event of the domestic court deciding that the killing was unintentional, the slayer had to be taken back to the refuge city.

---

*As when two men were felling trees and the head flew from the shaft and struck one of them.

This arrangement did not prohibit the waging of the blood feud against the unintentional slayer. It was only inside the refuge city that an act of vengeance was prohibited. If the avenger overtook the guilty party before he reached the bounds of the city of refuge, the law assumed him to have acted in legitimate zeal. The rights of the pursuer were not abrogated but only limited; and the justification conceded to passionate pursuit seems to have been looked at as a safety-valve of the violent reactions that demanded movement and relaxation.

It was very gradually that the law became emancipated from these savage and vehement passions which see a crime in every injury and attribute hostile intent to any action that appears to threaten mischief. " As the procedure to the word, so sentence sticks to the deed." Hödur's deed is, according to our ideas, an innocent accident. Yet, in spite of that, it must be avenged. In *Beowulf* there is the tragic figure of a father whose son has accidentally shot his brother, and who, unable to make up his mind to execute his second son as in duty bound, becomes melancholy and dies.

Many East African tribes practise the blood feud and, as a rule, no difference is made between intentional and accidental homicide.

There is no such thing as a blood feud within a group. Here the head of the family exercises his jurisdiction, as we shall see presently. According to a passage in Eusebius, which Post mentions, the ancient Parthians and Armenians did not prosecute a man who killed his wife, childless brother, unmarried sister, son or daughter. According to Islamic law the blood feud does not lie against a father who kills his son, although the law provides for his punishment. In East Africa it seems that the murder of a relation is generally compounded for a fine. Here, perhaps, though there may also be the remains of some religious sanction, the overruling consideration is that the killing of the murderer would constitute a further weakening of the group's strength. Similar ideas are to be found in modern civilized societies, among families of strong concentration, in the aristocracy and, to a certain extent, among the Jews. It is not apparently conceived that there is any occasion to render the offender incapable of further mischief, perhaps because the fatal encounter is usually the result of an isolated quarrel. Sometimes, as among the Arabs, the penalty includes a solemn ceremony of expulsion from the family, for should the expelled member afterwards be killed he would incur what the Arabs consider the dreadful fate of remaining unavenged. There is no doubt that in the story of Cain and Abel, the first-born who killed the more fortunate second-born, we have an illustration, not of the blood feud, but of the parlous state of one who, expelled by his race, has to leave his land and wander without the support of the group, in constant fear of being killed by anyone who chances to meet him. It was just because of this forlorn condition of his that God promised Cain His protection.

The Mosaic institution of cities of refuge was only one of the ways of modifying the rigour of the blood feud. Instead of a local restriction there might be a time limit. The Malays restrict the blood feud to twenty-four hours, three days, or a month after the deed, and often only to the moment after. But local restrictions appear as the more efficacious. During the time of the Franks it was forbidden to kill the offender in his own house; while since olden times a popular law protected him from his enemies with a special peace whilst in the

' Ding,' in the army, or in the neighbourhood of the king.

In the lynch law used in the case of persons taken *in flagrante delicto*, and in the summary justice of the ' called men ' who came running in answer to a cry and killed the offender caught red-handed, we see the blood feud losing its original character and passing into organized co-operation.

It says much for the tremendous strength of the blood feud, this mixture of self-defence and various legal conceptions, that not only does it constitute the basis of personal inviolability in present-day Africa and Polynesia, but that even in Europe remnants of it are preserved in Corsica and Albania. Various forms of the blood feud also reappear when peoples clash in war or classes in revolution: for when hostages are killed, the killing is directed, without any regard to individual guilt, against the enemy group.

Traces of a regulated blood feud are to be found even in the laws of the German States during the thirteenth, fourteenth and fifteenth centuries. The excited passions of the injured party are projected even into the demeanour of the judge: " The judge shall sit in the judge's chair like a grim-looking lion, and shall cross his right foot over his left, and consider the severe sentence and the judgment God will pronounce over him on the Last Day."

The idea that the execution of the law's sentence is the province of the State is of comparatively late development. To primitive societies it appears obvious that the successful prosecutor should execute the sentence he has obtained. " He whose goods have been stolen shall hang him "; so runs a clause of the treaty between Eiderstedt and Dithmarsch in 1417. Family solidarity, too, was a consideration that persisted to a late date. " On the first Monday in Lent, Claus Antonius, citizen of Budstatt, stabbed another citizen called Heinze Kirchern through the neck with a bread-knife while he was slumbering in the Ratskeller, where both were sitting at a feast. The latter fell without a sound and died painlessly. The culprit was immediately arrested, and the same evening, after the council had held three consecutive criminal courts, he was beheaded by the deceased's oldest kinsman by the light of straw torches."

Collective execution is even older than execution by the plaintiff. Either the entire group feels itself injured and threatened, or it opposes its solid united strength to the new threat of a blood feud, thereby breaking the endless chain of murder by force of numbers. The inhabitants of the village of Wiesenbrunn in Franconia, instead of delivering a thief up to the sheriff, hanged him, according to their ancient custom, from a tree, every man putting his hand to the rope. The antithesis of this conscious communal assumption of responsibility, which constitutes a shield for the individual, is the practice adopted in some parts of the United States of America. When a malefactor is to be hanged, three officials draw three levers, of which only one operates the drop, the others being ' dummies,' so that none knows who has been actually responsible for the killing.

In the Jewish code the primitive lynch law of the community was minutely organized, in the form of stoning, as a legal punishment. The chief witness had to cast the first stone at the victim. As the result of a long evolution in all modern legal codes, the personal factor has been eliminated as far as possible from the death penalty. Execution by means of electricity or gas is an example of the way in which human agency only presses a button and the forces of nature do the rest.

3. HOME DISCIPLINE

As well as its collective reaction to an external injury, the family group had originally an internal justice to safeguard its cohesion. It was only gradually that this decayed and was superseded by higher organizations. Such a discipline is rather contemptuously described by Homer as existing among the Cyclopes: " There there is neither law nor public meeting, but they all live on the top of high mountains in hollow rocks, and each judges his children and women as he pleases and pays no heed to the others." In this land where no shepherd drives his flock to pasture, where no plough goes through the earth there reigns only the family discipline of these giants who live solitary and unsociable. In a few powerful strokes Polyphemus is depicted as the type of primitive savage: " There lives a man of giant stature, who solitary always pastured them on remote meadows and never consorted with the others, but was intent on deceitful tricks."

Plato compares the dominion of the eldest of the family to the leadership of a flight of birds, and with all the optimism of his Utopian ideas calls the home the justest kingdom. And even Aristotle compares the dominion of the eldest of the family to that of the king. Like Plato, he cites the undeveloped social structure of the Cyclopes described by Homer as the fundamental form of family justice.

Within the circle of family discipline the wife was included among the chattels, like the slaves and concubines. The only restraint on the power of the master of the household over his wife, children and slaves was

29

his regard for their value as property and certain limits that very gradually were imposed on him by custom.

Under the original Roman law a woman could never be emancipated from authority; up to her marriage she was subject to the home discipline of her father, and then that of her husband began. The position of the Vestal, too, was similar to that of the ' Haustochter.' Even under the Empire the execution of a punishment decreed by the courts was sometimes delegated, " according to the ways of our fathers," to the offender's relations. Suetonius tells us that Tiberius " ordered that the relations of married women who led an immoral life and against whom no public accuser came forward, should intervene with family council and in accordance with the customs of the old republic." Tacitus reports the case of a well-born woman, Pomponia Græcina, who was accused of holding strange religious beliefs and whose husband was delegated to pass judgment upon her. Conforming to usage, he tried his wife for her life and honour in the presence of the relations, and found her not guilty. As Tacitus adds, it appears that the woman was subject to fits of depression, and for that reason was suspected of witchcraft. Many centuries before there had been discovered in Rome the secret society of the Bacchantes, which can well be compared to one of the medieval epidemics of witchcraft madness. After the discovery numerous persons were executed. According to Livy, " the condemned women were handed over to their relations or those in whose charge they were, in order that they should themselves carry out the sentence in private; should no one be found who was qualified to execute them, it was carried out publicly." This account of Livy indicates that private execution, however disagreeable the duty may have been, was regarded

as a concession to the family feelings which an execution
in the public market place would have outraged. The
tremendous tenacity of legal practices which have their
foundations in man's deepest feelings is illustrated by the
fact of acts of primitive home discipline surviving into
the German middle ages (walling in by the family, &c.).

In the Iliad, Zeus speaks of himself as exercising his
powers as head of the celestial household by tying up
and beating Hera (xv, 14-20).

> Thy arts have made the god-like Hector yield
> And driven his conquering squadrons from the field
> Canst thou, unhappy in thy wiles! withstand
> Our power immense, and brave the almighty hand?
> Hast thou forgot, when, bound and fixed on high,
> From the vast concave of the spangled sky,
> I hung thee trembling in a golden chain;
> And all the raging gods opposed in vain?

But the discipline of husband over wife was mitigated
earlier than the discipline of father over daughter. Over
the sexual purity of his daughter the father's eye watched
with an inexorable ferocity sharpened by jealousy.
Mommsen emphasizes that in historic times the
husband's power of punishing his wife at home had disappeared as an institution among the Romans, whereas
his powers over the daughter of the house, and above all
over a Vestal Virgin, continued until comparatively late.

One reason why the daughter was subjected to a much
stricter discipline than the son was probably her inferior
value as property. Further, in the daughter's case the
despotism of the head of the family may have been aggravated by male jealousy. But, whatever its origins, the
sentiment was of singular potency. The household of
Augustus affords one of the most tragic examples in
history. " The two Julias, his daughter and grand-

daughter, who had besmirched their reputation with every kind of excess, he banished. He had borne the loss of Caius and Lucius with more or less fortitude, but he let a deputy, the quæstor, inform the Senate and read out to them his judgment; and for a long time from shame refrained from all social intercourse. He even thought of having them executed; at least when at this time one of Julia's confidantes, a freed-woman called Phœbe, committed suicide by hanging herself, he remarked he wished he had been Phœbe's father.''

This prejudice against girls was evident from the moment of their birth. Between the ages of one and five considerably more girls than boys were killed. Whereas polygamy maintained the commercial value of women, the growth of monogamy tended to depreciate it, until, finally, the respective financial positions of father and son-in-law were reversed. The daughter from being an asset became a liability; for, instead of being paid for parting with her, the father had to pay a dowry to get rid of her. For a long time, however, there were to be found among the Germans signs of the former purchasing of women; the people of Dithmarschen still practised it in the fifteenth century. Brunner quotes the Dutch expression which even now describes the women as ' verkocht,' meaning ' verkauft ' (sold). Where, as among the ancient Jews, a girl was still regarded as an object of value, one can see that depreciation caused by an inclination to sexual freedom or by vows of sexual inactivity, would naturally be felt by the head of the household as an injury. Thus small economic value and impaired possessive value in a daughter both led to the same result—severe, even destructive, measures of home discipline.

A son's worst sins were disobedience to his father or

incest with his stepmother—the latter by no means an unlikely event in polygamous societies where the wife who grows old can easily be superseded by a younger. A decision of the son's against his father in favour of a stranger also constituted a criminal offence against the family interests. As primogeniture at one time conferred on the eldest son unlimited power over his brothers, as it does even to-day in dynastic families, fratricide was no unusual occurrence in the old rigid racial societies. The punishments which could be used were death, beating or expulsion from the family, a lighter form of which was the *relagatio* of Roman law. But Livy's vivid description of the exiled son of Manlius (nicknamed ' imperiosus ' or ' the domineering ') shows that by that time even the punishment of relegation was considered exceptionally severe. Marcus Pomponius expressly contrasts the care of dumb animals for their young with the brutal domestic tyranny of the human father, whose ire in the case of Manlius seems to have been aroused by nothing more than that his son had an impediment in his speech. From Livy's citation, however, we may infer that domestic discipline did not escape public scrutiny and that its abuse was severely criticized. In this connexion political passions and conflicts were largely instrumental in promoting more humane principles.

The execution of family discipline depending normally on physical strength, passed from father to son. The son became the master of his mother and sisters. Telemachus speaks very plainly to his mother; the woman has to be silent; the man is the master.

Quasi-punitive measures were forced on many peoples by the hard struggle for existence. There was, for example, the practice of killing old and useless persons.

33

PUNISHMENT

Traces of this are still to be found in the German legal antiquities. Among nomad peoples there also occur cases of compulsory suicide where the slowing-down of the march between two watering-places endangers the whole family. In a higher plane of culture, among agricultural peoples and those living in towns, the custom has disappeared.

The Mosaic law generally prescribed death for him who swore at or struck his parents. Youth shall stand up in the presence of a grey head and honour the old. In the Odyssey Telemachus hesitates to drive his mother from the house because such a violation of his duty would call down the vengeance of the gods.

That a brother kept his commanding rôle as head of the family even after his marriage is shown by a remarkable anecdote in Herodotus. Wife and children were subject to domestic discipline and so, *a fortiori*, were slaves. In early Roman times the *dominus* could do as he liked with human chattels. He could kill or torture them without let or hindrance. But nobody else could. The killing of another man's slave was damage to his property. Nevertheless, there is little doubt but the enactment of Antoninus Pius that a slave must not be punished severely without just cause (*sine causa*), only gave statutory force to what had long been a moral obligation of which the Censor took judicial notice. The slave who was fit for work was, like a son, protected by his economic value.

Should the head of the family be stricken and helpless from age, disease or accident, his failure was treated as a common danger, and he was deposed. Thus Chronos dethrones Uranos and Zeus in his turn drives out Chronos. Chronos in his fight for power rips off his father's genitals, which symbolizes that the old man

34

has lost his power of ruling and, by the same token, of protecting his family.

The idea of the old man rendered harmless is vividly given by Homer. Laertes, aged and forsaken, passes the evening of his days in Ithaca with only an old woman to care for him and idly shuffles about the vine lands. In another passage we have a description of the symptoms of senile imbecility which make the dethronement of an old man intelligible. He tends to associate with inferiors, servants and such like, and his habits degenerate. He neglects his person. In the summer he sleeps in the open on a bed of fallen leaves and mutters to himself.

The weak old man who is tired of life forfeits his position as a matter of course. The dominion of the father must be of use to the family. As soon as it begins to become dangerous, it is taken from him without scruple.

4. Ritual Origins of Punishment

Human Sacrifice

Public punishment originated in the conception of the offender as an enemy, either of the country, or, in a wider sense, of the country's gods, for which reason we find in civilized communities to this day religious ceremonies and symbols associated with the making and administration of the law. In many Continental countries the crucifix is still a solemn ornament of the courtroom, while in England the sittings of Parliament are opened with prayers, and assizes are preceded by divine service. Traces of the connexion are preserved in the classical idioms.

For long the oracle was used to provide proof where human wit was baffled, and among many negro tribes

35

it is still the only known psychological means for the detection of crime. In the rites which accompany the death penalty, we see clear indications of the sacrificial act that has been converted into legal punishment. The gods passed threateningly through the air, roaring not only at the disobedient member, but at his whole tribe, and the sacrificial surrender of the criminal, sometimes even of an innocent person, was an act of defence against a terrible common danger.

The indignation of the gods was not only an indication of human errancy but also of miscarriages of nature not due to the human will. The abortion is killed, and this destruction is not always without rational features. In 545 B.C., when Hasdrubal wanted to go to the help of Hannibal, all sorts of alarming omens had appeared to the Romans, and then: " Their spirits had hardly recovered from these threats from heaven when they were frightened by a new report that a child had been born in Frusino with the strength of a child of four; yet the strange thing about it was not its size but, like the one born two years before in Sinuessa, the uncertainty of its sex. The augurs who were summoned from Etruria declared that the creature was a revolting and repulsive monster, which must be banished from Roman territory and sunk in the sea, far from all contact with dry land. So it was stuffed alive into a chest, taken out to open sea, and thrown overboard."

Livy further relates the following from 552 B.C.: " From several districts comes news of revolting human and animal abortions. A child was born among the Sabines, and one could not tell whether it was male or female. Yet another was found, sixteen years old, also of uncertain sex. . . . All these phenomena were considered horrible anomalies, mistakes of a nature aberrating from one sex to the other in procreation. Hermaphrodites were abominated as specially evil omens and were immediately thrown into the sea; as had happened shortly before, in the consulship of Caius Claudius and Marcus Livius.''

Augustus banished his daughter Julia to Pandatoria, and his equally depraved granddaughter of the same name to the island of Trimerus, and Pliny tells us that it was the custom to maroon ' monstra ' on desert islands. The child to which his granddaughter gave birth after her condemnation, was at his command condemned to death by starvation as a ' monstrum.' In the Middle Ages we come across similar notions regarding the organically degenerate and the reaction of their expiatory surrender to the powers whose anger the abortion announced or called forth. The history of the persecution of witches belongs to the eternal *pogrom* by men and animals of anything that is ' different.'

Sacrifices were offered up as a thanksgiving to the gods: but also, in a world of secret dangers and timid weakness, in order to acquire or keep the favour of helpful powers. Thus one differentiates between thank-offerings and expiatory offerings; differences which are to be found again in the contents of the prayers. Precautionary acts or promises of sacrifice designed to anticipate the enmity of the gods are still found among us.

In early times battle and its issue was a decisive factor in life. Hence sacrifices were offered up before battle and particularly in the distress of a siege. A comparatively late and quite historical example of sacrifice to the god of battle is that of the slaughter of three Persian prisoners before the battle of Salamis. Plutarch's account makes a point of the cultural disparity between the scepticism of Themistocles and the superstitious terror of the mob: " Now when Themistocles was going to sacrifice near the admiral's ship, they brought to him three prisoners, people of exceptionally beautiful appearance as well as wearing magnificent clothes and gold ornaments. They were supposed to be the sons of Sandauke, a sister of the king, and Artyaktes. At the same moment as the augur Euphrantides caught sight of them the sacrificial fire burned up bright and high; at the same time somebody on the right sneezed, which also was an omen. So he stretched out his hand to Themistocles and bade him sacrifice the youths, killing them together after a preliminary prayer to ' raw-eating ' Dionysus. ' Then shall come both deliverance and victory to the Greeks.' Themistocles, however, was alarmed at the augur's significant and terrible speech. But—as is very common at decisive moments and in dangerous situations—the majority sought salvation rather from unintelligent things than from intelligent deliberation. They shouted to the god as with one voice, dragged the prisoners to the altar, and enforced the execution of the sacrifice according to the augur's spoken wish."

Tales of such sacrifices are commonplaces of the history of ancient civilization. They are to be found in the history of the children of Israel, in whose legal code the express prohibition of human sacrifice betrays a former use. They are continually to be found in Greek literature, and as happening not merely in legendary but in historic times. In moments of panic the apparently thick crust of rationality is rent by the subterranean passions of humanity, and (to change the metaphor) the favour of the deity is imagined as being knocked down to the highest bidder.

EVOLUTION OF PUNISHMENT

Even more fateful than battle was the struggle with the invisible enemy, pestilence. Grimm relates from a story of Afzelius: " In Västergötland they decided on a human sacrifice against the Digerdöd (the Black Death), and two poor beggar children, who had just come, were to be buried alive in the earth. Quickly they dug a trench, gave the children, who were hungry, buns with dripping, and made them sit down. While they ate the people shovelled the earth into the hole. ' Ach,' cried the smaller child, as the first shovelful was thrown over him, ' some earth has fallen on my bread and dripping.' The heap was thrown over them and nothing more was heard of them."

Like pestilence, famine might be averted by means of human sacrifice, which was used to force rainfall after a long drought. The springs begin to flow again when the deity is propitiated by a human sacrifice. The wind springs up from the smoke of human sacrifice, as we learn from the sacrifice of Iphigenia and a passage in Herodotus. According to the story, Menelaus is unable to leave the shores of Egypt because of adverse winds, so he sacrifices two children, who had been caught, and he sails away with a freshening wind. As the worth of what one receives is in proportion to the sacrifice, Hamilcar has several priests thrown to the sea god.

The sea is greedy and those who encroach on its domain without authority must propitiate it. For this reason many peoples used to make human sacrifices when they launched their ships. Sextus Pompeius, who imagined that he was Neptune's son, offered up a sacrifice of horses and, as some related, also men, to his father Neptune in thanks for the storm which had destroyed Cæsar's fleet. The sailors who had to bring Paul to Rome regarded the sea with all the superstition of their kind as a spirit which pursued murderers. This belief that the angry sea must have his victim still exists to-day. Wind and rain were things which southern peoples often lacked, and which they sought to charm into being. Battle, plague and the strength of a building were the chief cares of the Germanic and Slav peoples. Every building was an attack on the realm of the spirits who hovered round the land or river, and the more damage a collapse could do, as with castles, city walls and especially bridges, the more must the elemental powers be propitiated. Lambs, horses, pigs and hens were buried alive. The use of animals seems to be a modification of the usage which necessarily demanded human sacrifice. Grimm has compiled material on this subject collected from Nordic, Germanic and Slav sources. In a Thuringian saga a child was sold by its mother to be walled into the castle of Liebenstein in order to make it solid and invincible. According to the story, as it was being walled in, it ate a roll and called, " Mother, I can still see you," then later, " Mother, I still see a little of you," and as the last stone was put in place, " Mother, now I can no longer see you."

But human sacrifice early entered upon a slow process of transmutation into wider, different substitutive shapes and forms. There is only one certain trace of human sacrifice in Vedic times—at the building of an altar. Here five sacrificial animals are said to have been used; man, horse, ox, ram and goat, each is for different gods. The heads were built into the lowest layer of the stone work. Man gradually disappeared from this form of building sacrifice, which, according to Indian sources, was in use in the not too distant past. Actual human sacrifice slowly changed into the offering up of human symbols such as dolls, or into symbolical killing, such

40

as beating till bleeding occurred and other procedures in which wounds were inflicted. But before the substitution of actual dolls made from straw or wax (Egypt) or any other material, useless human beings were sacrificed, *e.g.*, old people whose exposure combined a good riddance to the community with a gift to the gods. We know of one example from Roman history. After the decrepit people, whose age in those troubled and warlike times was not greatly respected, came slaves, and finally criminals. A further mitigation of the old complete process was symbolical killing as a sacrifice and substitutive acts by which blood had to flow. The sacrifice finally dissolved into ecstatic self-mutilation in which form it is still preserved by many Eastern sects.

Finally, animals took the place of men, although there is some divergence of opinion on this point. It is possible that animal sacrifice was the primitive rite and that human sacrifice was a development. Perhaps there have even been cycles of sacrificial practice that we can no longer trace. At first, it is true, animals took their place with men, for primitive thought makes no great difference between men and animals; even to-day a child thinks of animals in a fairy story as human. The Indo-Germanic peoples seem to have considered the horse, especially, as a beautiful, useful and in many ways superior relation. We have just mentioned Sextus Pompeius, who is said to have sacrificed to Neptune horses and, as is said, men at the same time. In Scandinavia horses' heads, cut off and stuck on stakes, were turned with open jaws in the direction from which the enemy was expected. The Romans saw on the old battle-field of the Teutonburg Forest horses which had been sacrificed and whose heads were nailed to trees, and

41

human sacrifices. In India, too, we find the combination of man and horse as superior sacrificial animals.

Apart from the altar-building ceremony, to which reference has been made above, we have in the Vedic era two closely connected forms of horse-and-man sacrifice. In the first case the victim who was " a white, yellow-eyed, wrinkled, leprous, crippled and sexually impotent man " from the high-born Brahman family of Atri was drowned; in the second case the human sacrifice, richly adorned, was strangled with his own red garment.

In the ' magical ' phase of human thought death was conceived as committing all the forces of the sacrifice to the elements; as man reflected, feared and prayed to gods, the sacrificer approached the personified deity in the capacity of giver, appeaser, and at the same time even expiator. Blood was and is a special fluid, and the blood of a sacrifice the very highest power. The primitive idea is by no means extinct to-day. The practice of magic and the act of sacrifice still live in our penal laws. If we wish to make criminal punishment practical and efficient, we must do with it as we have done with the art of healing—purge it of ' magical ' conceptions and make it a victorious method of preserving life.

Decapitation

Mommsen brings forward philological evidence to show the great age of this form of execution. In early Roman times, as appears from the account of the beheading of Brutus's son, the hands of the sufferer were tied behind his back; he was stripped, bound to a stake, and scourged, then thrown to the ground and his head cut off with a blow from an axe. Mommsen is of opinion that this corresponds exactly with the procedure at the sacrificial slaughter of animals. The religious significance of the stake has still to be ascertained, although there is a variety of material from Indian, Egyptian and American religious history awaiting compilation. The Osiris of Busiris was originally a wooden stake. On a stone coffin in the Berlin Museum the holy stake has arms, clothes and a crown. The Indians of Brazil plant a stake in the ground, which constitutes their divinity, and to which they bring sacrifices.

Since earliest times the executioner's axe has been the emblem of unlimited official power, and it can hardly be called a coincidence that the death penalty has returned to Italy at the same time as an ancient Roman symbol. In historical times such executions were only ordered by a dictator. Livy gives a very clear description of how the Romans, faced with the bared axe of the dictator Titus Lartius, became afraid " for now there is nothing for it but to obey." The fasces of the lictors displayed the instruments of sacrifice : axe and rods with a blood-red thong holding them together. In the symbol of the power of life and death was incorporated the extreme concentration of the State's claim to sovereign authority.

We know from sculptures as well as from old written records that the procedure in sacrificing an animal was first to stun it with a blow from an axe, and then to cut its throat. On the whole, methods of animal slaughter have not changed much in the course of centuries. With men this combination of stunning and bleeding was not necessary, because, for anatomical reasons, a simple blow from the axe was sufficient. There are some very clear accounts of the ancient procedure. Suetonius describes Caligula's morbid parapraxis when, as sacrificial slaughterer, with his sleeves rolled back, he stepped up to the altar, swung the axe on high and struck dead his assistant, the knifer, who was standing near him. Elsewhere, among the stories of evil omens of Galba's fate, Suetonius tells how an ox, which was to have been slaughtered in the emperor's honour, maddened by the blow from the axe, tore itself loose and rushed up to the emperor's chariot, drenching him with blood.

The custom of not executing death sentences on holy days, which is still observed, is also reminiscent of the sacrifice. Wilda mentions a similar West-Gothic rule, and adds that the Christians' God is a merciful God, for in heathen times great feast days had been regarded as specially appropriate for gratifying the deity with the sacrifice of evil-doers. This supposition can hardly be applied to the Roman culture. Suetonius relates with disgust that the mad Tiberius, who did not worry much about the gods and their worship, never let the executioners have a holiday, not even on festivals. Even at the New Year festival many death sentences were carried out.

Nocturnal executions, like noctural sacrifices, are sacrilege. " Is there a more infamous deed than a nocturnal execution? " says Seneca indignantly.

The place of the axe was taken in military usage by the sword. When Germanicus reached the old battle-field of the Teutonburg Forest he came across gallows and ' graves.' To die by the sword was for the Roman a soldier's death, and Arminius, who had himself served in the enemy ranks, was only copying their military justice. The grave originated chiefly in the execution of military justice, partly in a recollection of the sacrificial ditch, the gate of death, but it was also calculated to spare the soldier's honour, by avoiding a lengthy exposure of the body, such as there was with hanging.

44

EVOLUTION OF PUNISHMENT

The custom of forcing people to dig their own graves has been preserved in the usage of modern war and civil-war. But why the unclothing which was prescribed for Roman decapitations, which the sacrificial priest himself carried out and which we shall come across again in most methods of execution? We are no longer clearly conscious of the denuding of the sacrifice, because of the countless pictures of the crucifixion which we see in churches and streets. " Nakedness," says Wuttke, " is more frequently a requisite of magical performances than of acts of religious origin." In another place he remarks, " With the stripping off of the body's covering, there falls, too, the envelope of the soul, of fate and the secret everyday life; there is positive poetry in it, and it has in many respects a significance similar to the prostitution of virginity practised in many heathen religions. Nakedness is requisite not only for divination, but also for discovering buried treasure and when taking precautions against ghosts, witches and sickness, for rogatory feasts, sacrifices to attain fertility and for love spells."

The heathen Arabs walked round the Kaaba completely naked and it was not until Mohammed's law that the pilgrim's dress was introduced. One may observe the remnants of such ritual nakedness in the penances of the church in the Middle Ages. The sinners appeared at the Cathedral door " bareheaded, with bare feet and the body covered with a sack."

The religious character of decapitation was equally marked among the Germans, who used it in sacrifices of animals, when the head was stuck up on a pole, a tree, or a building. Even the infuriated mob in the French Revolution unconsciously followed this custom which it copied from French official justice. The Germanic con-

querors of Varus having captured some men and horses
sacrificed them and fastened up the heads of the horses
near the place, and the civilized Romans could scarcely
deplore this custom, for about the same time a similar
human sacrifice was made according to ancient ritual
in Rome itself. " And the noise did not abate," says
Cassius Dio, " till Cæsar stepped quickly among them,
seized one with his own hand and killed him. This
one got his due, but it was not enough, and two others
were slaughtered as an atoning sacrifice. I cannot
give the reason for it, the Sibyl had not spoken it, nor
was it announced by any other god. They were
slaughtered on the Campus Martius by the High Priests
and the Priests of Mars, and their heads stuck up before
the Regia Martis." It is quite clear that the mutinous
soldier was thus sacrificed to the god of battle as well as
to military discipline. The Priest of Mars slew him and
gave up his head to the god.

For many peoples the axe was not only an instrument
of execution, but also an attribute of a deity, an object
of worship and a sacrificial implement. It is to the god
of the clouds, of the storm and lightning, that the victim
belongs. The figure in the old saga of the rider on a
white horse who, with a broad hat, " but often without
a head and on a headless horse," galloped along, reminds
us of this Wotan, whose predecessor, Donar, a rougher
and more primitive kind of deity, drove with his rolling
wagon through the clouds, swinging his hammer or axe
and with it cleaving the hills.

So Amira was really right when he expressed the
thought that it was for the god of lightning that the
head was stuck up on a pole, so that he could come
flaming down and consume his offering. Just as our
ancestors consecrated horses' heads to their deity, the

human head is offered up and with it, the seat of higher life, the most precious part of man, his soul. Man's primitive faith still seems to suspect the possibility of life in a motionless body as long as the head remains unsevered. The soldier who, seeing Galba, who had been stabbed, lying on the ground, cut off his head, had the dim feeling that not till he had separated head and trunk would he have, once and for all, destroyed the former emperor and made certain of his successor's thanks. The unclothing of the victim which is still partially carried out at modern beheadings, is also a preparation for sacrifice.

The practice of the cock-shy still persists at Easter and during the Carnival. " Among Slavs and Germans the cock was a sacrificial animal, the animal of Swantewit, the greatest Slav god." In this a cock is either decapitated or beaten to death, according to the district. In Southern Bohemia on the occasion of the first marriage during the Carnival a cock is dressed in a red cape, solemnly condemned to death and bound to a stool; the bystanders, begging its forgiveness, behead it—to the strains of funereal music, after which it is roasted and eaten.

There is a curious form of the belief in ghosts, the vampire superstition, prevalent in some German and even more in Slav districts. In the border provinces of Eastern Germany vampires are called ' after-consumers ' or ' blood-suckers.' They are described as being: " people who are born on certain unlucky days, which cannot be exactly ascertained, who keep a fresh colour after death, or have the left eye open and in this way keep for a long time in the grave." These people still have a kind of life which they use against those who are left behind, and when an epidemic broke out

47

the spread of the deadly sickness was obviously put down to the activities of such a ' vampire.' This vampire is rendered harmless if its head be cut off. So we see that life is assumed as long as the corporeal connexion between the trunk and the soul's container, *i.e.*, the head, remains unbroken.

The Middle Ages took up the struggle against the old heathen ideas of sacrifice without becoming intrinsically their master. Capital punishment still kept a supernatural reference. The only change was that the criminal now became a person possessed of devils that could be attacked by the destruction of their fleshly abode. With the ascendancy of Christian ideas the old sacrificial axe was thrust into the background. Such experimental departures from the heathen implement, as execution by sledge-hammer or broad-axe, did not, in general, last long. More and more the sword was used after the manner of Roman military justice. The axe, as the weapon of the old, beaten gods, became the more infamous the less it was used, whereas death by the sword was honourable and a privilege, so much so that it was regarded as suitable to be recorded on the tombstones of those who suffered it. When the French revolutionaries introduced the guillotine, one of the motives behind the innovation was hatred of class distinctions in punishment—especially the aristocratic privilege of execution by the sword.

Breaking on the Wheel

Breaking on the wheel was pre-eminently the punishment for murder. There can be hardly any doubt of its origin as a religious rite. The culprit having been securely bound, his limbs were broken with a wheel, after which the living body was bound to the wheel and wheel

48

and body were raised on an upright. A procedure so elaborate and involved implies deep historical roots. Grimm suggests that the pounding with the wheel was a later development, and that originally the execution was carried out by driving wagons over the body as is still sometimes done in India. In a later development the culprit was bound on the wheel itself in the first place and his limbs were broken with some instrument such as a cudgel or club.

The further back one goes the more symbolic the wheel becomes. For the Germans, as for the Greeks, the wheel was an obvious symbol of the sun, and it has maintained its position in popular superstition with great tenacity. The stork, a sacred bird, and like all red animals (foxes, squirrels and robin redbreasts) sacred to the god of lightning, protects one from fire from heaven which is the reason why it is allowed to nest in our villages on a wagon wheel. At the celebration of the solstice in many districts of Germany wheels are erected on posts and set alight; or burning wheels are rolled down a mountain. A story from East Prussia tells of a curious custom which dates back to remote antiquity. "In the evening when all the fires have been put out, an oak post is erected in the ground and on this a wheel is revolved until it catches fire. From its flames sticks are lit and with these new fires are lit in the houses."

For breaking on the wheel the wheel must be new and have nine or ten spokes. The victim must be left on the wheel until his body disintegrates. No one dare deprive the deity of his property, for originally the wheel was a punishment with an element of chance; he who survived it, that is to say, who was still alive after some three nights, was allowed succour. The deity had rejected the offering.

49

Thus the explanation that in breaking a person on the wheel sacrifice is made to the sun god is obvious. In breaking on the wheel, the wheel with the body on it was erected on a pole, stretched up to the deity so that it might take the human life and be appeased. This is hardly intelligible except as the persistence of an old sacrificial rite. It cannot be explained by the later idea of its having a deterrent effect.

This interpretation is also supported by the Ixion myth of the ancient Greeks. Ixion had spilt ' not without malice ' the blood of his relations, throwing his father-in-law, who had promised him rich wedding presents, into a fire-trench which was covered over with twigs and dust. Then raving and ' drunk with nectar ' (Lucian. Dialog. deor. 6, 2 pp.) he demanded Hera. Zeus played a trick on his love so that, instead of his mistress, he embraced a cloud. In punishment for his mad demand Ixion was bound to a glowing wheel and driven round the earth in an eternal whirl, the first great murderer of Greek mythology . . . Odin is one-eyed, god of the clouds and the storm, but also master of the stars and the sun, which is his eye and with which he looks over every country, just like Helios in Homer. Animals and men are sacrificed to him and to him, who promotes and watches over man's moral communal life, law-breakers are surrendered. Round every bloody structure with its wheel circle the ravens, Odin's sacred birds, which whisper to him all they see and hear.

So much for the wheel part of the procedure. What of the breaking part? Why was this particular mode of inflicting a lingering death considered an exceptionally heavy punishment? Historians of crime have not sufficiently considered this point. The answer is probably to be found in the importance which ancient belief attached to the integrity of the bones. The graugans involved a certain type of wound, the marrow wound. A fracture of the lower or upper extremities was considered equivalent to a wound which went to the brain. German popular justice had a curious method of reckoning the atonement to be made for splintering the bone; the penalty was fixed according to whether the bone, when thrown from a distance of 12 or 24 feet over the road on to a shield, gave out a clang. Likewise there appears in Jewish law and in the Gospel of St. John a very old idea, which regards the skeleton as the permanent abode of life; unless the skeleton is intact resurrection is impossible. In this connexion Rochholz relates a story from German mythology: "The god Thor comes driving with his two he-goats up to the peasant Egill; he kills the goats for his supper and allows the peasant and his children to join him; but they must throw the bones they gnaw unbroken into the goatskins. The peasant's son Thialfi is greedy for the marrow, breaks open a thigh-bone with his knife and sucks it out. In the morning Thor takes his hammer, sanctifies the bones in the animals' skins and resurrects the goats, but one of them runs lame in a hind leg." A custom of the Bushmen seems also to point to the belief that life resides in the marrow and is finally destroyed with its crushing. "Feared men, not women, sometimes sorcerers, who had a pernicious influence, and others whom one had had to fear while they were alive, were securely tied up before burial in the specified squatting position with thongs of animal skin; then in many cases their backs were broken with a stone or axe."

If, then, the forces of life, propagation and resurrection were believed to lie in the marrow of the bones, we can understand the damage and destruction which was wrought on the future life of the man who broke a person's bone. He was crippled and mangled, in reality ' cut to the quick ' for all time. As up to the present no other explanation has been given, the hypothesis I put forward here will not be without its use to science.

The singing, and above all the bleeding bone in the saga (S. Mailly, 193) is a last remnant of the belief in the bone as the seat of a concentrated and ' hardy ' life.

Hanging

In the geography of crime the use of hanging as a method of execution has curious boundaries. It was not used at all by the Jews, and only slightly by the Romans, and there is little mention of it among the Greeks. Is the inference that the inhabitants of the sunny and comparatively windless climate of the Mediterranean, where the wind is regarded as a refreshing, and not as a deadly and threatening element, would not be likely to practice a form of sacrifice that is associated with the fury of the powers of the air?

Hanging is practised in the Steppes on the borders of Europe and Asia (whence the Turks may well have got this punishment), in middle and north Europe, and in North America, whose first settlers introduced it from England. Grimm demonstrates from the philological standpoint how the abundance of poetic expressions for hanging testifies to its widespread use. No punishment occurs more often in the Edda, where we also find passages which make its sacrificial character clear. In ' Starkad's Rœckblick ' King Wikar is supposed to be offered up in a mock sacrifice to Thor, the god of the wind. He is hung from a tree and symbolically sacrificed by a scratch from a spear. But Starkad treacherously kills the king. The same practice is mentioned again in the runic poem of Odin, where Odin says: "I know that I hung on a windy tree nine nights long, wounded by the javelin; dedicated to Odin, I to myself, on that tree whose origin no one knows."

In Switzerland in olden days the gallows was usually called the 'wagende Studen,' and Osenbrüggen quotes Campbell's description of a mound in Graubünden which was called 'chünettas,' probably derived from Cunabula, in which one can see a play on the rocking motion of the hanged. We can only recognize the religious character of the punishment when we take into consideration the most important attendant elements, the offering to wind and storm and the fastening to a tree.

Even woodcuts of the Sachsenspiegel represent the wind as heads or faces in the act of blowing. The imagination of the Germans and Slavs especially has peopled heaven with personifications of the wind and storm; in the form of the 'Wind Bride' there is still a personification of the element in our language and ideas. At any rate, the storm was imagined as a greedy monster, an insatiable evil demon who went out to plunder and who had to be pacified with gifts.

Remnants of this dim belief are preserved in our superstition. In practically every part of Germany, when a wild storm is raging, they say that someone has hanged himself. The devil, Odin's Christianized successor, drives off with the soul of the hanged and the storm does not abate until the corpse is under ground. They believe in Bohemia that hanged criminals also make storms, and in this connexion Wuttke says: "This may be connected with the fact that men were hanged as sacrifices to Woden. The storm-god receives the souls."

The unbroken life-force of the hanged flows over into his clothes, the gallows, nail and the rope, and all relics from one who has been hanged bring luck " for a sacrifice which has been consecrated and offered to the gods is considered a source of prosperity." Abhorrence of the evildoer, which comes from fear, is commuted after his consecration and elevation by death, into the magical power of one who has crossed the mortal boundaries.

The gallows must stand on an eminence or on the shore, with the winds blowing round it. It was perhaps not only to serve as a warning that it was built close to the border, which gave rise to all sorts of quarrels between neighbouring lands. It was a crime to remove a person from the gallows not only when he escaped alive, but also if he was already dead. The hanged had to be abandoned to the winds until he was completely decomposed or the ravens had eaten him. Odin's thoughts and messengers go about the world in the shape of ravens. " He flies through the air in the shape of a raven, alights on the gallows and accepts the offering made to him." Amira gives a fine description of the simultaneous hanging of men and dogs. For Odin is the god of the forest and the chase, and the dog is his favourite animal. In the old legend of the wild huntsman who rages through the sky during the spring and autumn storms, baying hounds, which many see as fiery dogs, run with him. These are the lightning which stabs across the heavens. The old custom of sacrificing dogs was continued longest at the hanging of Jews, and Hans Fehr quotes a story from Schaffhausen (1585), about some peasants whose dogs had been taken away for the execution of a Jew, and who were determined to have them back: one of them even offered the judge his best cow, but this was refused. The dogs remained alive for six or seven days beside the Jew who was hung up by his legs with his head down.

The Jew is supposed to have existed three days longer and to have spoken with his wife and children.

Grimm has collected much material about our forefathers' sacred groves and trees. As late as in the eleventh century, Unwan, Bishop of Bremen, had to have such woods forcibly uprooted. Sacrificial animals hung on the sacred trees, as even to-day birds of prey are hung over the doors of barns or horses' skulls fastened on the roofs. The most honoured of the sacred trees was the oak, which with the hazel was ' left in peace,' that is to say, they were not to be cut down. Even the Greeks believed that there were higher beings living in trees, especially in the oak, and their belief was adopted by the Roman mythological poets.

It was on such a sacred tree, usually the oak, but sometimes, too, the willow, that criminals were hung. This was the tree on which, according to Tacitus, the old Germans used to hang traitors and deserters. At the celebration of an Indian sacrificial feast, not unlike our All Souls, the remains of the sacrificial cakes were thrown into the air, picked up again, and hung high up in two baskets attached to the ends of a beam ; as a roadside meal for the dangerous god Rudra, who brings wind, storm, pestilence and fever, so that he might pass by without doing any damage.

The tree had to be leafless and withered, for the tree, on which a man is hung or hangs himself, dries up. The miasma of the crime penetrates it like a disease, and for that reason the unexpected breaking into leaf of a gallows was taken as proof of innocence. The gallows had to face the north, and I cannot agree with Grimm when he compares this to the *arbor infelix* of the Romans. The German gods lived in the north, while from the south in the last decisive struggle of the Germanic cosmogony, came the destroying powers of the fire world, and from the east came the frost giants. For this reason we must regard the north side of everything as the side on which the glance of the gods falls first, as is to-day still the presumption in the superstition of banishing sickness. The north is not horrible, but the direction of heaven to which the heathen turns in his prayers. It was the Christians who first brought the north into disrepute as being the quarter where the heathen gods had their palaces.

The gallows was for preference erected at cross-roads. Although the tree must not sprout, the branch must not be rotten or bend, and the rope or withe had to be new; for should the branch or rope break, the culprit was none the less deemed to have paid his penalty. The deity had refused the offering. Throughout the Middle Ages there runs a contradictory praxis of justice in regard to these poor sinners whom chance released from death. The new rope was supposed to have magical properties, as Samson reveals to Delilah (Judges xvi, 11), in that it makes one weak, like cutting the hair.

Later the branches of the oak were replaced by the artificial tree, the gallows. According to an ancient source the trunk which was used must not have a knot hole nor must anything be nailed to it. Even to-day oak is the only wood that may be used. Later several kinds of stone gallows were employed. Sometimes when the criminal was caught red-handed a gable-end served the purpose.

Originally the culprit was always naked, but later he was left with his shirt, as pre-war pictures from Russia show. Women were seldom hanged. A woman who was hanged in 1619 was, for the sake of decency, dressed in a pair of trousers with her shift over them. The removal of the body of Mary Blandy, who was hanged on 6th March, 1752, gave rise to a scandal.*

What was originally death from exhaustion by being bound up became later a combination of hanging and strangling. In this connexion the covering of the eyes is of very ancient date, being mentioned in the Twelve Tables, and in one place Cicero says: " The head covered with a cap of wolf-skin." Was the head veiled to turn aside the criminal's evil eye, the strongest and most imperceptible kind of magic? Here we have no sure authority on which to rely; but we know that the dead person's eyes must be closed immediately, for if one eye remained open a relative would soon die. If the dead person's eyes are not closed he drags another after him.

The criminal psychologist may observe how often an otherwise callous murderer will carefully cover the face of the corpse; here, too, the belief in the vengeful power of the evil eye continues to have an unconscious effect. The dying Cæsar covered his face with his toga. From this, as well as from the story that Nero's death seemed so terrible because his eyes protruded far from their sockets, one may conclude that the Romans were accustomed to close the eyes of their dead.

But sometimes even the murderer wears a mask, like the executioner in the Middle Ages, and this is not only to guard against recognition; for in the old custom of the cock-shy the bystanders are blindfold when they kill the animal.

As I have already said the superstition that a severe storm means that someone has hanged himself, is spread over all central Europe. The Tritopators of the Athenians, souls of their ancestors, were at the same

---

* See the " Trial of Mary Blandy," Notable British Trials Series, William Hodge & Co., London.

time spirits of the wind. " The spirits there are in the wind, are souls become free." Is there any connexion with the Marsyas legend? According to Gruppe, Marsyas was a Phrygian demon with the features of Silenus. Silenus belongs to the wind deities, and Gruppe is thinking of an ancient wind magic. In old pictures Marsyas is seen hung up by his hands. The flaying of the living person is a later explanation of the artist's habit of painting Sileni on a leather bottle as demons of wells and the wind.

To be hanged was a disgrace. The length of the exposure was ignominious and one was additionally shamed by being stripped. One can thus understand how bitterly King Gunther in the Nibelungenlied felt his defeat, and particularly his being hanged on, of all times, his wedding night, which should have proved his strength. With this disgrace of the king's begins a development which, to cover up the king's disgrace and weakness ended by " fell into the flowers Kriemhilden's man," and finally with the extirpation of the entire Burgundian royal family.

Crucifixion

Crucifixion, especially in its original form, is closely related to hanging. This method of punishment, though found in Roman criminal law and religious history, was not native to Rome but borrowed from Asia. Its origin lies perhaps in the clear inclination of primitive peoples not actively to bring about death, but to let the deadly forces of nature take their course by hindering the living organism's mechanism of flight and defence. In its origin crucifixion was probably killing by exposure to the sun, even perhaps by thirst, which could not have been thought of in the cloudy northern climate, but would readily occur to men's minds in the shadowless south.

Crucifixion was not, originally at least, carried out quite in the form which the Church has made traditional and which has given us the cross as the symbol of Christianity. There was certainly not always a cross beam, the sufferer being simply tied to a post, as is shown by the Greek word for cross, ' stauros,' whose strict meaning is a stake or pole. In Justinian, out of respect for the religious symbol, the word ' furca ' is substituted for ' crux,' which leaves it doubtful whether this already constituted the change over to hanging or the name for another form of crucifixion, of equally ancient origin, was borrowed.

We meet this ' fork ' in the clear description of the fugitive Nero's death. When he heard that the Senate had outlawed him, and were searching for him, he who had executed so many, asked what sort of punishment ' according to our fathers' way ' was. When he heard that it was to be shut naked in a fork and whipped to death, in his horror he seized two daggers, tried their points and then, an actor to the last, sheathed them again.

Crucifixion was considered a particularly horrible method of punishment, and for that reason was treated by Justinian's jurists as the *summum supplicium*. The only punishments which can be compared to it are burning and being thrown to the wild beasts. Again and again the severity and brutality of this punishment are emphasized; as when Galba ordered it in the case of a guardian, who had poisoned his ward, and when even Domitian shrank from inflicting it when the cowardly Senate had decreed it according to ancient custom as the punishment for *lèse-majesté*.

The long duration of suffering is evident in the New Testament. Jesus speaks with the criminals who are hung beside him, and also speaks to His mother, her sister and the disciples. The Jews did not anticipate a quick death and asked Pilate to allow the legs of those on the cross to be broken, for a man on the cross is " cursed in the sight of God " and profanes the land. According to old Jewish custom, the bodies must be taken from the trees at nightfall, and either covered with a heap of stones or buried.

The Punic general Bomilcar was crucified by his own people because he wished to go over with the army to Agathocles. He showed such intrepid courage that from his cross, like from a platform, he reproached the Carthaginians with their sins, and it was not till he had spoken in loud tones to the crowds, which had quickly gathered, that he died. The punishment was thus not immediately deadly. Claudius, who liked now and again to see an old-fashioned punishment, waited a whole day beside the criminals, who were bound to the stake, until towards evening the executioner at last arrived. He wanted to watch the expressions of the dying men, as at the Gladiatorial Games. Crucifixion was followed by scourging, but this could also precede it. In the gospels we see stripping and scourging as the preliminary to crucifixion. Josephus tries to prove Florus's madness by relating how he had men of knightly rank scourged in front of his chair, and then nailed to the cross. According to Mommsen the condemned person was stripped, his head covered up, as was done for hanging, and then the fork was put on his neck; his arms were bound to either side of the fork, which was then, with the body fastened to it, pulled up on a post to which the feet too were bound. Thus crucified the criminal was scourged. A very slow and lingering death followed. In the gospel Jesus complains expressly that He is thirsty; and when a cry escapes him the bystanders' first thought is that he is tortured with thirst.

This scourging, to which we to-day attribute the clear and simple purpose of giving pain, has a quite different significance when we remember a certain ritual of mourning which is found throughout the world. In Athens, Solon was the first to forbid physical expressions of grief, such as scratching one's cheeks and beating one's head and breast. At Indian burials the women dance around weeping, with disordered hair and beat their hands against their breasts and thighs. Painful scourgings occur during the puberty rites of every race; e.g., the Spartan rites, where clearly they could not have had the character of a punishment.

In the same way we know of priests of many periods of civilization scourging or even emasculating themselves. In two places St. Matthew mentions that scourging was practised in the Jewish synagogues.

All these customs are only understandable if they are connected with a movement of dismissal, ' beating off ' of evil powers. Beating is an energetic form of throwing away, shaking or brushing off. A clear explanation of the custom is given in a Vedic source: " We beat the evil away from you." At the Indian ceremony of consecrating the king, the priests beat the newly annointed ruler, and a number of well-known customs occur to us, the accolade, the priest's blow at confirmation; the light blow on the cheek given by the Carinthian peasant to his new prince, and the box-on-the-ear which children were given at the ceremony of ' beating the bounds.'

According to this view, scourging is repulsing, expiatory cleansing from noxious substances, older and magically more powerful than the death penalty itself, which it so often introduces or accompanies. The infliction of pain is a secondary development.

In Mommsen's opinion religious connexions are not so evident in crucifixion as in decapitation. But, all the same, some mystical effect was attributed to the cross, quite apart from its close relationship with the older punishment of hanging. Pliny quotes an old peasant superstition that a nail or rope from a cross was possessed of as much healing power as wood which had been struck by lightning. Evidence on the point is scanty, but it may be conjectured that the supposed healing quality was connected with the old sacrificial idea that his lasting life force and the favour of the appeased deity hover round the material which killed him. Thus in the Christian conception the cross has redeveloped a sacred symbolism, in which the deity sacrifices his dearest to himself. Its sacred character is, perhaps, not discoverable, but in the course of the centuries was won from this way of dying and still bears it to-day.

It is difficult to say whether hanging and crucifixion are based on those forms of defensive magic which were used in India against dangerous impurities. In one place in the Vedic texts the different classes of the buried are mentioned: those buried in a grave, those thrown away and those exposed. Unlucky things were ' exhibited ' on a tree, but the meaning of this word is too confused for us to be able to draw sure conclusions.

Stoning

Stoning has its origin in the grey dawn of time. In Euripides the men of Tauris shower stones on the departing ship. In Homer the wrathful Hector says to Paris: " If the Trojans weren't cowards, they would long ago have fitted you with a dress of stones." Herodotus, too, often speaks of stoning. The Athenians threw stones at Thrasyllus because he had concluded an unfavourable armistice. He succeeded in saving his life at an altar, but his fortune was confiscated.

This, the first and most terrible weapon of man and apes, with which Hector broke open the gate of the Greek encampment, plays a large part in Greek mythology. The primitive giants, who were destroyed by the gods, were heroic and uncultured savages who, like the raging Polyphemus, fought with tree trunks and rocks against the modern armament technique of the gods, Zeus' lightning and the arrows of Hercules, and by which they were defeated. In ancient art they are regularly depicted as slinging stones. Between a weapon and a means of punishing there is the closest relation.

From Jesus' words: " He that is without sin among you, let him first cast a stone at her " (St. John viii, 7), and from other places in the New Testament every child knows that stoning was the ceremonial death penalty of the Jews. It was the punishment for blasphemy, and had Judea in Christ's time not been under Roman rule and subject to Roman laws, perhaps the symbol of Christianity would have been not the cross but a cairn.

In the old Mosaic law stoning is prescribed for all crimes which arouse the anger of God, and which could withdraw his protective hand from the people. In face of a common threat, the people, by collectively repelling and destroying the criminal, banished the danger of this.

In theocracy the worst crime is idolatry, high treason against God's state. Here, too, the proof and the procedure were simplified, the depositions of two or three witnesses, but not of one, being sufficient for judgment of death. In order to furnish the summary procedure with summary guarantees, the witnesses had to cast the first stones.

The crime of idolatry was so threatening and horrifying that it severed every tie of kith and friendship. In the event of their being seduced to false beliefs, the pious were supposed to be forced to denounce brother or son, daughter, wife, or best friend and to cast the first stone at them. It seems that only mother, father, and husband were excluded from this deadly circle.

In the Jews' prescription of the death penalty for making human sacrifice (an oft-repeated and thus very practical admonition indeed) the threat of death, itself a kind of sacrificial act, was directed against the altars of divine competitors. For the stoning of such sinners, Moses had arranged a shortened procedure which was materially different from the orderly progress of the judicial procedure. In such cases the duty of the chief witnesses for the prosecution to throw the first stone was omitted.

Stoning was the punishment for breaking the Sabbath, into which the Pharisees tried to tempt Jesus; and the man who gathered firewood on the Sabbath has taken refuge in the shadows of the moon and German fairy stories. God is questioned about the Sabbath-breaker who gathered wood, and his answer affirms the criminal's purpose. In cases of negligence a substitute sacrifice was made instead of the man, which was graduated according to his means and in a highly social way went from two turtle doves to a handful of meal. If ordinary punishment was decided on, then the substitute sacrifice was omitted.

We know from the story of the woman taken in

adultery (John viii, 7) that stoning was prescribed as its punishment. It was also the punishment of homosexuals and for lying with animals, and of the priest's daughter who prostituted herself. It is true that the law speaks of burning, but one must admit that Michaelis is right in his supposition that the stoning was aggravated by subsequent burning.

How can we connect the form of the punishment with its ritual? The West Asiatic Semitics make this comparatively simple. In Egypt, Syria, Phœnicia and Palestine we see more or less highly developed forms of an ancient stone cult. Rough stone altars, which were worshipped as divine, stand in Bethel, Garizim, and Jerusalem: one dimly imagines that the deity takes up his abode in the stone on which he receives prayers and offerings.

Although our knowledge of old Arabic mythical conceptions is very imperfect, still we do know that the Arabs worshipped stones and rocks; those were the gods of the stone age, of which the Egyptian use of a stone knife still reminds us. v. Kremer, in his treatise, describes many such stone deities; they were blocks of archaic stone; one was the red rock and two others were called white. In Petra, quite near the border of the Holy Land, stood the sanctuary of the stone god Dusares. In the temple a block of unhewn stone lay on a base of gold, and over it the blood of the sacrificed animals was poured. v. Kremer, in explanation of this usage, supposes that stone was taken to be worshipped because it was the hardest and most imperishable material, from which weapons and instruments were made. On the other hand, meteoric stones, by apparently falling from heaven, naturally caused fear and evoked veneration, which is the human soul's means of defence. At any rate, we come across such deified stones also in Greece. The magically defensive effect of stone is evident in Indian rites, similar to holy water, the clod and the tree.

Later the crudity of the idea disappeared, a spiritualized image of God was separated from the visible object, and thus the refined cult still kept the ancient symbol. The holy stone in the Kaaba and the sacred stone salver in the Omar Mosque at Jerusalem are, and remain, relics of the ancient stone worship, to which only new ideas and cultural feelings have been added, without the age-old seat of religious emotion having suffered any change.

The cairns which were erected by the Israelites over people who had been executed, as well as those which we find at the burial of Ethiopians and those which, tremendously magnified, rise over the burial chambers of the kings of Egypt, cannot be dissociated from the tendency of those peoples towards stone worship. In Corsica, which s formerly conquered by the Carthaginians, a Semitic people, it is, according to travellers, the custom to erect a cairn at the spot where someone has been murdered, on to which everyone who passes throws a stone. In Syria and Egypt there still perists the custom of putting up two stones in pyramid form as a sign of a visit. In the old Jewish cemetery in Prague a similar custom may be observed. Plato's punishment for the patricide was that he should be killed by the executioner's assistants, and thrown naked on a certain cross-roads far from the town, whither the authorities and every member of the community brought in the State's name a stone, a curse armed with gravity, and cast it at the corpse's head.

The most sacred oath of the Romans, " *per Jovem*

lapidem," was taken in the open air. He who took the oath held a stone in his hand and, after striking down the sacrificial animal, said: " If I wilfully deceive, then may the father of light, protecting citadel and town, cast me out of house and home, like this stone." It was with this ritual that the solemn pact between Rome and Alba was sealed. Holding a stone in his hand Hannibal promised Italy's slaves their freedom and the soldiers the surrounding country, and again, much later, Sulla thought to keep Cinna faithful by making him swear this most solemn oath: with this object Cinna went to the Capitol, and with a stone in his hand swore the oath, even adding curses against himself; that should he not remain faithful in his friendly sentiments towards Sulla, then let him be cast out of the city, as he now cast the stone from his hand.

Stoning as a legal punishment is unknown in Roman law, but it is known as a form of lynch justice which, at times of great excitement, was called forth even against the gods and their temples. It appears sporadically in the Germanic penal codes only to disappear again from criminal law, being preserved only in lynch law.

In Swedish sources stoning, pelting with clods or killing with rubble stones appears as the punishment of women. This is closely related to burial alive, especially when one remembers that the condemned person, like a tree about to be planted, is put in a grave-like hollow. In a Swedish painting of as early as 1300 one sees the criminal with bandaged eyes. This mode of execution has many peculiarities. At times the missile was accompanied by a curse. Wilda describes an old form of stoning which was particularly ignominious, but admitted of escape with God's grace. In Norway anyone who committed a theft in the country or town was a ' gauntlet ' thief. His hair was to be shorn, his head smeared with tar and plastered with feathers. Then the people formed a passage through which the thief was driven towards the forest and everyone had to throw stones and pointed sticks at him, a civic duty which it was a criminal offence to neglect. This running of the gauntlet was the latest form of this collective punishment, and only came to an end when spears were no longer used as weapons. As with the old Nordic communal punishment there was a remote possibility of escaping from the passage alive, in which case the penalty was considered paid and the crime pardoned.

It is said that in Iceland a conical cairn is erected over the body of an evil-doer. In many of the older pictures there is already a regular hillock over the person who has been stoned. According to the Schwabenspiegel, to have stones piled over her is the punishment for the wife who is no longer pure. Here one can see the connexion with the feminine punishment of burial.

Probably stoning masses meant to cast off the pollution of a crime, the stone being the vehicle of charming away the noxious substance and driving it back to the transgressor. Later on ideas of sacrifice replaced the magic rite of stoning. Although its connexion with ancient sacrificial rites has been obliterated, we cannot refuse to admit it. The Germanic gods, heroes and giants lived on large rocks, mountains and cliffs, whose names they took. Even to-day the first person to climb dangerous faces and rocks erects a cairn on the top, a sacrifice to the mountain spirit which has spared him. There still goes about such a one, Rübezahl, a queer and moody demon of the mountains, who, vengeful towards those who insult and despise him, shows himself friendly towards good people and helps the poor. He is clearly a perversion of the heathen god Wotan. In the Tyrol when a child makes his first ascent of Burgeisen, he must pick up a stone and throw it on to the cairn under which the ' wild-maid ' lives, and in doing this must say : " I sacrifice, I sacrifice to the wild maid." In the Urschelberg at Pfullingen (Swabia) there is a deep cleft, the ' nightmaids' hole,' and every passer-by throws a stone into it and says : " We, too, wish to bring an offering to the nightmaids," otherwise some misfortune happens to him on his way.

In the legends of the kings of Untersberg, near Salzburg, Kyffhäuser and Odenberg, in Hessen, and in the legends of the Hörselberg, newer conceptions are mixed with the old, faded pictures of the gods : just as magic powers used to haunt smaller stones, so in the bowels of the mountain sits the old father of the gods; the ravens which fly about the mountain are his birds.

The punishment of stoning has disappeared from the penal code, but it persisted tenaciously in mob justice and even to-day reappears when the people riot. Hans Fehr has reproduced a picture from the Zurich Central Library. The executioner has made himself drunk and can no longer strike an accurate blow with his sword. He has struck one of the condemned in the back and the other in the shoulder. The people revolt against this. They turn to the people's ancient weapon, and stone the executioner to death.

In most large German cities in the Middle Ages there occurred similar attacks on clumsy executioners. This mob justice took hold of the executioner as of a sacrifice which was its by right. " So the executioner especially is liable to be killed for any miscarriage in an execution and no order to keep the peace nor any threat of punishment can counteract this view," says Knapp, the historian of Nürnberg's penal law. The psychological explanation of the primitive rage of these outbursts is that the act of execution itself has loosed the killing instinct of the masses, which now, freed from old inhibitions, comes to the surface; should it not be satisfied by the execution, or should a clumsy blow during the execution excite the people's sympathy, then the loosened destructive urge turns against the executioner himself. In all these happenings, so often retold, there lies a lesson on the deleterious effect of the death penalty, an absolute refutation of its purely intimidatory effect, which no one will, or can, dispute.

The Germanic Middle Ages introduced modifications of the death penalty which increased in mildness until, finally, they were reduced to symbolic acts—the wearing of the osier-rope or halter, similarly the carrying of a dog, as substitutes for the penalty of the gallows, carrying a wheel instead of being broken on it; and, finally, the carrying of a stone as a symbol of stoning.

The punishment of ill-tempered and quarrelsome women was the ' scolding-stone ' to which the people gave many humorous nick-names. A few such stones have been preserved; according to Mailly one hangs in iron bands from a pillar in St. Peter's at Salzburg. Later the single stone was sometimes made into a woman's head with the tongue stuck out and a clasp in front of the mouth.

For wearing the ' stone-of-vice ' those days on which crowds collected were selected, the weekly or yearly market days and also Sunday. " In Memmingen the woman had to carry ' the stone-of-vice ' from one gate of the town to the other, on a Sunday when the bells were ringing for mass" ; she could, however, buy exemption for a pound of hellers. According to the records of Schaffhausen in 1503, a woman there had to carry the

70

' stone-of-vice ' because she had kept money which she had found.

In Nürnberg the stone was the punishment of women guilty of deceit, match-making, gambling, slander and blasphemy. Since 1485 it was also specified for back-sliding adulteresses.

The shape of many punishment stones which are pre-served in Swedish town houses, according to Grimm, supports the conclusion that in punishing adultery the drastic form of a Priapus was chosen.

Drowning

One cannot say that water was without religious ritual significance for the ancient Jews. Both Egyptians and Hebrews had the religious ritual of cleansing, which, because of the shortage of water, was carried out by a slight sprinkling with holy water. Salt water had a con-centrated cleansing effect. The Christian baptism is a later development of this old ceremony of purification. The symbolic bath of Christ constitutes the beginning of this development which to-day is softened down to the dogma of rebirth.

In a country which, like the Judean Highlands, has little water, there were practical objections to drowning as a death penalty. In ancient Rome, on the other hand, which was situated on a navigable river, and where, as in Greece, many springs were objects of religious venera-tion, the punishment of drowning had a very clearly defined procedure.

In Roman law drowning as a punishment must be accessory to the country's expiation by the ' procuratio,' the cleansing act of sacrifice; if a monster with its threats of disaster appeared in the world, it must be annulled and washed away by sinking it in water. In an important

71

passage Seneca says : " We avoid mad dogs, we kill bad-tempered and wild oxen, we sink our steel into a sick bullock, so that the herd does not become infected, we destroy abortions and drown in deep water children who are weak and unnaturally formed . . ." So the actively damaging tendency of the mad dog is compared to the threatening power of the abortion. The patricide is thrown into the expiating water, as the evil creature is drowned to protect the community.

According to Mommsen the origin of the punishment of drowning people in a sack was the idea that every life-bestowing element—water, air and earth—should be removed from the criminal and that he should be sent into the company of the wild creatures of the forest. For this reason he was tied up with every kind of animal, snakes, cocks, dogs and even apes; but this hypothesis is hardly satisfactory. He was scourged with red rods; over his head a covering of wolf-skin (or the uterus of a she-wolf) was drawn; wooden soles were fastened on to his feet and he was sewn into an ox-hide sack, driven in a wagon drawn by black oxen to the shore of the sea or river and thrown into the water. This punishment was only inflicted on confessed patricides. I do not dare to judge as to whether the wooden shoes were meant to be a kind of fettering as Mommsen supposes, that is to say, a kind of stocks, or an execution toilette which would reduce the condemned to the level of the beasts. The old sources which mention drowning leave us in the dark.

Patricide was regarded as an action contrary to nature. This misshapen creature was to be got rid of and wiped out. The land must be freed immediately from the contaminating presence of such a monster, before the anger of the gods struck him together with his innocent fellow-citizens.

Claudius had Caligula's chest of poisons sunk in the sea as a malign abortion of a diseased mind; and we often come across drowning, or at least throwing into the water, as the last stage in another execution. The cleansing effect of washing is known from Christ's trial. The Greeks, as well as the Romans, held the opinion that water from a spring or the open sea washed away guilt.

This belief, as old as man himself, is associated with another. The movement of water, whether of a river or the sea, gives all primitive peoples the idea that it is animate. In the sea, lakes and waters dwell demons, who demand sacrifices. Animal sacrifices are due to the river whirlpools. According to Agathias the Alamanni sacrificed horses to the streams and gorges; horses and oxen were offered alive to the Scamander, and in olden days the Argives sank ready bridled horses in the Argolic water Dine for Poseidon. At the time of the Gothic war the Franks, when crossing the River Po, sacrificed to the water demon, throwing their prisoners, women and children of the Goths, into the water. It was chiefly the Alamanni and Franks who worshipped rivers and springs. One prayed on the river bank, lit lights and set down sacrificial offerings. According to Plutarch's story, the Gauls lost courage because the holy women advised against a battle before the new moon. These prophetesses watched the heaving and rushing of the waters and prophesied, expounding the moving water. Such spirits of the streams guard faithfully what has been given into their keeping, as the Rhine guards the treasure of the Nibelungs. The Goths buried their beloved king Alaric under the waves of the river, which they had drained and diverted over the body.

PUNISHMENT

In German superstition there are clear traces of the idea that the force of water is alive, greedy for power and revenge. In order to pacify the waters and their sprites, who demand a victim every year, in the Bodetal they throw a black hen into the water; in Westphalia fruit and bread, and in the Neckar valley a loaf. Children's clothes are also thrown into the flood. According to Wuttke, even at the beginning of this century many of the country people of North Bohemia went on St. Veit's day (15th June), the men carrying black cocks and the women black hens, into the Riesengebirge to the seven springs of the Elbe at the foot of the Schneeberg, where they let the cocks loose in the woods, but drowned the hens and in doing so knelt and prayed; with the water they brought back they washed their oxen. In Hessen on 24th June the springs are hung with garlands, the people dance round them, begging them to continue to give water. At Christmas one looks into the springs with lights, glittering sacrifices. In the Tyrol the elements— air, earth and water—are fed like hungry living beings, whose satisfaction one wishes to win. Goethe's fisherman pictures with great artistry the superstition about the dweller of the deep who hunts beautiful human children and lets them recover their health in his arms. Here poetic expression has been given to the attraction which water exercises on many sickly people who are inclined to suicide. I call to mind Conrad Ferdinand Meyer, whose mother committed suicide by drowning herself and for whom water always had an inexplicable attraction.

Many popular customs, as Grimm relates them from Hesse, or Burchard of Worms from the Middle Rhine, are sacrifices to the thunder god Donar; the nakedness of the young girls who make the sacrifice points to the

74

act of worship. Every Catholic country has rain processions.

It will certainly put our criminal-historical ideas on a foundation of inner understanding, which only the association of ideas can give, and not of purely dug-up learning, if we anticipate a little here and examine the question why, in middle and north Europe, drowning was essentially a woman's punishment. It cannot have been only for reasons of decency, as is frequently put forward, that ' shooting ' into the water was substituted for breaking on the wheel and hanging. Articles 159 and 166 of the Carolina expressly specify execution by the rope for men and by water for women.

Oldenberg says that in India " the waters are conceived as mothers, waters from heaven, running waters, those dug up and those which appeared of themselves, the clear purifying waters and those straining to the sea. They have in themselves every remedy, they wash away all evil and guilt." On German ground the springs were brought into being by a miracle, by lightning, lance or sword falling from heaven; by a blow with a wand, the pawing of a horse's hoof, the rooting of swine or of a dragon. Spirits live in these bubbling gates to the underworld. " The spirits of the springs are predominantly feminine "—and Weinhold adds that even the names of the German rivers, in so far as they are of German origin, are feminine. The people bring offerings to these nymphs of the springs and waterwomen; human beings, a black cock; later, in place of living people, straw-dolls, flowers, cakes, gold rings, even needles and nails. But the old festival of the Brunnenfege is solemnized by the girls of the place in the dark, with prayer and song. No man may be present—thus, even in ancient times, nakedness of the virgins was possible and required. Women who were to be punished were given over to the feminine spirits of the water, that is to sister elements, to the ' mothers ' of the Indian legend, who took the condemned into their lap, drew them down and away and absolved them. Not till this idea faded did men sometimes penetrate into the circle of this punishment. The sacrificial character of drowning, the recognized and hallowed refusal of the victim by a deity, if the river threw the condemned out again alive, is evident in the old ordeal by cold water.

When Ludwig the German marched against Charles the Bald, who was disputing his inheritance, he had the right or wrong of his cause decided beforehand by a trial by ordeal. Ten men underwent the ordeal by hot water, ten carried the glowing iron and ten submitted themselves to the ordeal by cold water. During this the army knelt and prayed to God to declare by his judgment whether the West Frankish king, Charles the Bald, ought to get a larger piece of the disputed Lorraine than he already possessed or be satisfied with what he had. After the ordeal all thirty men were found to be unscathed.

In the ordeal by cold water the accused was thrown into the water with a rope round his body. If he floated he was guilty; if he sank he was innocent. The ordeal by water was used especially to try witches and sorceresses. The Inquisitors' *Institoris* and Sprenger disallowed ordeal by fire in the case of witches, because with fire the devil can protect them from hurt.

There was an old ignominious practice, well-known in Merry England, which Grimm calls the ' water ducking.' But, according to the graugans, anyone who pushed another into water, liquids meant for food or drink, or urine or excrement, was submitted also to this punishment. Such an injury was not punished simply because it endangered life. According to the Friesians' ideas, it was an insult or a peculiar hurt to be sprinkled with water. From all this one must draw the conclusion that certain injurious powers were secretly operative in fluids. Perhaps the dark custom of the water-bird belongs here, in which the recollection of an old water deity may well persist.

The punishment of drowning, apart from the spring cult, came to the Germanic peoples from the north, from the shores of the sea. At the sea the condemned was pushed out beyond the breakers. The use of the punishment spread from the sea along the big rivers into the hinterland. The execution was usually carried out from a bridge (St. Nepomuk in Prague).

Originally the perpetrator was stripped, bound and his eyes bandaged or a sack was pulled over his head. In order to make it easier for him to sink, stones, sometimes mill-stones, were hung around his neck. In old Nürnberg the punishment of drowning fell into disuse owing to the shallowness of the Pegnitz and its liability to be frozen in winter, but in Basel it was for long the customary capital punishment for women. As a punishment for men it was used only in cases of bigamy and ill-treatment of parents, in accordance with the Roman practice. The process of execution in Basel was mild. The condemned person was led on to the middle of the Rhine bridge, his hands and feet were bound together, two inflated ox bladders were tied to his neck and feet, and then he was thrown into the river. Sometimes the fishermen who were waiting for him by the St. Thomas Tower were able to pull the delinquent out of the water still alive, in which case he was given his life. The fact that the water had thrown the man up again alive was taken as a sign that the deity had rejected the offering.

A harsher form of this punishment was to sink the person in a barrel stuck with knives, while a substantial mitigation of it was ' Schwemmen,' a form of ducking in which the condemned person was drawn for a little through the water by a rope. This juridical usage was common in Switzerland and Alsace. In Schaffhausen in 1564 a mother was drowned for immorality and her daughter drawn through the water (' geschwemmt ').

Besides these usages we know from Friesian law of the rites which preceded the execution of a desecrator of a temple. His ears were slit and he was castrated.

One may therefore conclude that drowning, too, originated as a sacrificial act. The people sacrificed the criminal to the demons which lived in the springs, rivers and the sea. For the very reason that in drowning the rescue of the perpetrator was regarded as refusal on the part of the deity, one can say that the old heathen belief lingered far into Christian times.

A different form of drowning, reminiscent of one of old forms of burial, was to put the condemned person into a leaking boat without mast or sail. This punishment is only found in sagas and folk songs, and reminds us of Frazer's chapter on the expulsion of evils.

The partly destructive, partly cleansing function of water is brought back into our minds, when at the conclusion of another form of execution, burning, the criminal's ashes are flung into a river. That was what happened to Huss. Originally women were only drowned for theft or sorcery. Agnes Bernauer was accused of sorcery and on 12th October, 1435, drowned in the Danube at Straubing. (In this connexion it is perhaps not without significance that drowning is the favourite mode of suicide among women, and also of infanticide. May there not be some substance in the old notion, which we find

78

embodied in many myths and superstitions, that there is a real affinity of the feminine organism with the temperamental and restless element?)

In the Middle Ages suicides were put into barrels and allowed to drift down stream. In Frankfurt a warning to the finder, " Let it drift," was written on the barrel.

Burning

Fire, more than the other elements, possesses a Janus head. It is now beneficent, now destructive. It casts man out of one emotional sphere to another. Geographical circumstances, too, play an important part in determining the kind of regard in which it is held. To the Icelander the glow of a fire is something quite different from what it is to a Persian. In countries where volcanic upheavals are frequent, the people show a stronger tendency to deify the destructive forces of the earth's interior than the inhabitants of the vast Steppes and regions of volcanic inactivity. No element changes its form more than fire; it strikes down from the clouds as lightning; breaks in flames from the heaving ground; lives in stones from which it can be struck and sleeps in the wood, which, under the rubbing of skilful hands, emits the fiery particle.

The religions of the last three thousand years are deviations from horrible, rough forms of worship of earlier times. The more terrible the fire-god seemed to antiquity, the richer in offerings was his service. He it was who was most severely hit by the reaction when new religions began to overcome the old and bring them into contempt. The fire deities were now degraded into demons, crippled and cowed, but still rebellious, brooding over and hankering after their former power. Their kingdom became the place of punishment in the after life (Hades, Hell), while other earlier conceptions of future punishment disappeared. The remnants of their ancient majesty were appropriated by the new gods Ormuzd, Jupiter, Jehovah and Allah. Dim recollections of powers worshipped with fire persist in superstition with a tenacity which points, not to their dying out naturally, but to a forcible suppression of the ancient cult. For what another's hand has killed, is not dead.

It is clear from all this that burning has a twin sacrificial significance; in the first place, it is a question of sacrificing to the fiery element, conceived as a greedy and consuming deity, as in the cults of the great volcanic countries of Mexico and Peru, of the Phœnicians and Carthaginians and of those peoples who adopted their customs and ideas. Later, with the victorious advance of Christianity, new ideas arose; sacrifices were still burned, but they were burned in honour of a victor and now death is brought by the element which has sunk from sanctity to perdition and whose intrinsic nature is the destruction of others coupled with the consumption of self.

In the Middle Ages burning was the punishment of complete extermination, drawing an impassable barrier between the perpetrator and the people. Crimes which most roused the anger of the gods—heresy, witchcraft, incest and sodomy—were expiated on the pyre. The suicide, too, was burned to ashes and his ' powder strewn on water, thrown on cross-roads or even on the gallows. Finally, the names of those who had been burned were perpetuated in the roll of outlaws. In all this, expression is given to the aim of absolute destruction and sequestration in relation to the deed.

The new rite, in order to overcome the old gods, turned back to the ideas which preceded them. The

80

sacrificial fire had been preceded by the magical fire, which we still find in many forms in the Vedic ritual. " The function, which is indeed fire's oldest function in religious services and which usually occurs among even the most savage peoples, has been preserved in the Vedic Agni: that of effectively burning up and defending against evil spirits and all hostile magic. With his sharp, bright eyes he sees the hidden demons, seizes them with his tongue, with his brazen teeth . . .," says Oldenberg. In the Middle Ages the burning of heretics and witches was connected in the minds of the judges with the old idea of fire as the element which kills and drives out demons, and it was with this basis conception that ingredients of new beliefs and purposes, sacrificial offering and deterrent punishment, were mixed.

The Jews did not use burning as a punishment, but only as a *post-mortem* ignominy; the importance of differentiating their cult from those of the neighbouring Baal-worshippers precluded its use as a means of execution. But burnt-offerings are mentioned continually in the history of the Jews, the rising smoke being believed the most direct way for petitions and gifts to scale the celestial vault. In the face of very grave danger a Moabite king seized his eldest son, the heir to the throne, and so his dearest possession, slaughtered him on the city wall and offered him as a burnt-offering to the gods. The Israelites, however, feel that he has won over his diety and bound him to make a return, and withdraw. In another place it is related that the Babylonians roasted Zedekiah and Ahab in the fire. There is also the story of Shadrach, Meshach and Abednego, whom the burning fiery furnace was unable to harm and to whom, after so magical a preservation, King Nebuchadnezzar gave high posts. From mythical times we have the story of the burnt-offering which Abraham, at his God's command, was going to make of his only son Isaac, but for whom a ram was substituted at the crucial moment.

The custom of sacrificing to the fire god came to Carthage from Phœnicia. " At Carthage there was a metal statue of Chronos in a stooping position with hands stretched outwards and upwards. It was heated red hot by a stove placed under it and then the children who had been chosen as sacrifices were laid in its arms from which they rolled dying and with convulsions, which one took for smiles, into the fiery gullet." In Egypt, too, we come across human burnt-offerings, from which we can understand how the Jews took with them, from the land of their oppression, their horror of burning. Manetho relates that " In the city of Eileithyia it was customary in the dog days to burn alive some so-called Typhonians, that means red-haired people, and to strew their ashes in the air with shovels." According to Diodorus Siculus, since ancient times people of the same colour as Typhon (red) were sacrificed by the kings at Osiris's grave.

At the end of the Iliad, Homer tells how a colossal catafalque was erected for Patroclus, and in addition to the usual sacrificial animals, jars filled with honey and oil; four horses, two dogs and twelve Trojan prisoners were killed and thrown into the glowing furnace. Throughout the night Achilles kept pouring wine from a golden jug on to the flames while a storm of wind, whipped up by Iris, fanned the blaze. Patroclus' spirit had told Achilles in his sleep that his soul would not find rest till the barrow rose high above him. Cremation was for the Greeks the passage to Elysium; on the other hand, the thought of being eaten by dogs was unbearable, as also was that of being buried in river-mud, or being eaten by eels. As Agamemnon says, to be cremated is " to expiate with fire."

An entirely different conception, which can only be explained by the difference in the form of worship, appears in one of Herodotus's stories (iii, 16). " As soon as he (Cambyses) had entered the royal tower of Amasis, he ordered Amasis' corpse to be taken out of its vault. And when his order had been executed, he had the corpse flayed, its hair torn out, and stabbed and mishandled in various ways; and as the people laboured at this in vain, because the corpse, being embalmed, was tough and would not fall to pieces, Cambyses gave the order for it to be burned, which was an impious command. For the Persians regard fire as a god. Hence the burning of a corpse was not customary with either people; with the Persians, as is stated, for the reason that they regard it unjust to assign a human corpse to a god; with the Egyptians, however, fire was regarded as a living animal which consumed everything it got and which, when it had satisfied itself with its food, is destroyed together with that which it consumed."

In Rome the worship of an old fire deity, Vesta, continued till the end of the fourth century A.D. In the temple of Vesta burned the eternal fire whose extinction was regarded as a national catastrophe. The eternal fire was watched over by the Vestals, an order of priestesses which Numa is supposed to have founded.

The principal mode of disposal of the dead among the Romans was cremation; Suetonius gives an impressive picture of how the Roman people made Julius Cæsar's funeral pyre out of the magistrates' chairs, women's jewellery and children's clothes and fired it; then with the funeral torches they rushed from the obsequies to the murderers' houses. Hence in Roman law death by burning was at first only known as a " reflected " punishment of arson, he who set house or granary on fire having to lose his life in the same way. According to Mommsen the criminal was stripped, nailed or bound to a post which was then pulled up off the ground and a brushwood fire lit underneath, by means of which the delinquent was killed. When the terrible fire, which Nero is supposed to have kindled, broke out in Rome, and the ancient sanctuary of the goddess of the moon and the temple of Vesta were reduced to ashes, Nero had those people who were loathed on account of their depravity and commonly called Christians denounced as the perpetrators and subjected to the severest punishments. As incendiaries they were, according to the formal law, clothed with animal skins and torn by dogs or nailed to the cross. To be thrown to the dogs was the punishment of anyone who deserted to the enemy. The Christian dissenters were, as incendiaries, nailed to the cross, lifted up for the fire to be lit under them and burned.

Burning passed in Roman law for a very severe punishment and occurred to the tumultuous mobs when they wanted to give vent to their most passionate hate.

" An undergarment smeared and interwoven with inflammable material," a kind of Nessus shirt like that which the jealous Deianira sent to Hercules before he mounted the pile on the summit of Œta, served to increase the severity of the punishment. In another place, Juvenal mentions the pierced breast, clearly referring to the stake which was driven through the middle of the body and came out again at the mouth. One should not overlook the fact that Tacitus mentions the burning of revolutionary Christians in the same place as he tells of the sacrifices made by Nero after his consultation of the Sibylline books. Among those gods whom Nero made it his business to propitiate after the catastrophe of the fire was Vulcan, ' mulciber,' the god who brings fire to life and strokes and appeases the evil creature, and who is also the god of fire. It was a terrifying portent when St. Elmo's Fire played round the head of Vulcan's statue. One may also presume that the reflected punishment of burning in the Law of the Twelve Tables had developed out of an ancient sacrifice whose meaning has been lost. In the Roman penal code arson was put on a par with murder and brought into a curious relation, which can be explained by political experiences, with rebellion. Livy tells of such a trial for arson in which ' hereditary enemies,' Capuans, were condemned and executed.

The Germanic conception of punishment by fire must start from the crime of arson. We do not know exactly why it was considered ignominious to be injured by fire or to meet one's death in it. In the isolated settlements of olden days the danger to the community was less, but the danger to the householder must have been greater owing to the lack of fire-fighting organization and the inflammable material of the houses; even to-day the same feeling of being direly threatened runs in the peasant's veins. Arson, secret and violent, but especially nocturnal arson, was considered the greatest delict of all. A number of peoples who, when they emerged into the light of history, did not replace the death penalty by other defensive systems, have prescribed death by burning as the punishment for arson. In Anglo-Saxon law arson belongs to the most serious category of crimes, with open murder and treachery to one's master. To die in the flames was considered ignominious. The vengeful mind of Kriemhilde intended this shameful death for the Burgundians, when she ordered the hall to be set on fire.

I doubt whether, according to Salic law, sorcery and

poisoning were punishable by burning, for the fire penalty is only to be found in the Wolfenbüttler Codex of Salic law. There is a similar lack of clearness in regard to the law of upper Sweden for, according to East Gothic laws, the sorceress was to be stoned. At any rate, the medieval custom of burning heretics has, for obvious reasons, no primary connexion with pagan methods of punishment. The conception of fire as cleansing and demon-destructive is a relapse to pre-religious conceptions and came to Christianity from the East. '' The Son of Man shall send forth his angels, and they shall gather out of His kingdom all things that offend, and them which do iniquity; and shall cast them into a furnace of fire ''; (St. Matthew xiii, 41-42). The punishing fire is an eminently Judæo-Christian idea, taken from the scorching sun of the Orient, which would make little appeal to the peoples of the north. Christ's furnace of fire is the ' eternal torment ' to which the wicked shall be banished at the last judgment. Deeper strata underlie the later employment of the fire penalty in cases of religious and moral offences. First comes fire as a defence against demons and destroyer of evil spirits; then follows a stratum of a religious character, which has been effaced or appears in other legal customs, but which has been comparatively well preserved in superstition. Such legal forms are laying waste and ordeal by fire. On the other hand, I can see in the fire-penalty so frequently used at the end of the Middle Ages no pure descendant of the old Germanic or Roman sacrificial punishment, but a cross between magic fire and Oriental ideas. The religious punishment of hell is brought down to earth and executed in anticipation on the sinners.

And now a word about laying waste with fire and the ordeal by fire. Even to-day in the anger of the masses there is the impulse to destroy the enemy's house; to pull it down, to burn it. As well as the rational purpose of making it impossible for the outlaw to remain there, there is also the idea that the evil-doer's possessions have been infected by him, are harmful and ' tabu ' and must be cleared away like dead cattle or the criminal himself. In most cases this is served by burning them, which is well known from the later Germanic Middle Ages and goes back to hoary antiquity. Whenever the burning constituted a danger for the neighbouring houses, the house was pulled down; sometimes it was even removed to a safe place and there burned, so strong a hold had the old religious method of destruction by fire and breaking. Professor His tells us that, according to the Brokmerbrief of the thirteenth century, it was prohibited to take anything away from the places of destruction, everything had to be destroyed and removed from human contact.

Ordeal by fire, too, is inexplicable save on the supposition that the pious believed that the deity was present in the fire or working by its means. The accused walked over red-hot ploughshares, held red-hot iron in the bare hand or clothed only in a shirt (according to tradition a shirt of wax), passed through a blazing fire. The divine fire is of such ancient pagan origin that Christianity had to fight a long and often, to all appearance, a losing battle against the deeply rooted juridical belief in it. To-day we still speak of putting one's hand into the fire for something or of going through fire for someone, without suspecting the pagan origin of the expression. As modern language has not preserved anything similar from the other kinds of ordeal, one is justified in concluding that divine judgment and trial by fire were the most deeply rooted.

At the burning, the condemned person was stripped, bound and shorn (like the Vestals). Amira is of the opinion that this can very easily be regarded as a ritual act, because the fire is supposed to consume the soul of the criminal and prevent it from floating about and committing further harm. I think that in saying this Amira has confused the old form of sacrifice of Egyptian, Phœnician, Roman and Germanic law with the Christian burning of heretics. In the Middle Ages, when witches, sorceresses, suicides, homosexuals and incestuous people were burned, it was with the idea of exterminating both body and soul, or, at least, to send and frighten the soul very far away by the blaze that sprang up. That this complete extermination was clearly intended we know from the frequent burnings of Jews and witches and from the fact that their ashes were strewn to the four winds. On the other hand, the old sacrificial punishment did not see in fire the essentially evil element of pure negation and destruction, but a deity, now well wishing, now angry, who accepted and consumed his gifts in a rush of flame.

All doubt about our forefathers having practised primitive fire sacrifices disappears when other non-penal strata are considered. At the end of time the life of mankind goes out in a colossal sacrificial fire, as a similar fate comes to the individual. Disposal of the dead by fire, which is mentioned by Tacitus, appears in Cæsar as a form of sacrifice. Here the gods are asked by the casting of lots, whether they will accept the prisoners at once. In Tacitus's time the Germans were given horses with them on their funeral pyre; on Baldur's pyre were placed his wife Nanna, who had died of grief, and his horse; a dwarf who ran at Thor's feet, and Odin's precious ring. (Note the striking similarity to Patroclus's funeral.) The sacrificial character of the action appears clearly behind the belief that in the underworld the hero must have within his reach horse, servant, falcon, weapons, jewels and wife. This sacrifice has persisted to the present day, for among many peoples at the harvest festival, on Shrove Tuesday, at Easter and Midsummer Day, the people burn animals, cats and squirrels alive.

A symbolic burning of men is the burning of straw dolls, partly in a ritual form from which women were excluded, and above all the strewing of the ashes on running water.

Sacrificial gifts to fire appear very often in Germanic superstition. In Carinthia food is offered to the wind and fire in order to make them friendly. If one throws ham, lard and other foods into the fire it protects the house from fire. Fire is put out by throwing into it a tri-coloured cat (upper Palatinate). The Slavs especially have preserved the remnants of the worship of fire. In Bohemia one is supposed to throw something into the fire before every course. In Steigerwald when fire breaks out, cakes, shaped like men and baked at Christmas or the New Year, are thrown into the flames, which thereupon go out.

The eternal lamp of Christian churches is red, an artificial, small and tamed fire of adoration.

Burial Alive

In making a distinction between burning and burying, we have, in strictness, been guilty of an inaccuracy. Actually there has always only been burying, which was once preceded by burning, but which was otherwise carried out without any preliminary destruction by fire. The burial of the dead could never be detached from geographical conditions and the customs of the people, though religious ideas played their part; thus where animals were revered as the images of the deity, one could not see anything wrong in throwing the dead to the messenger of the gods for their acceptance. It was quite different with peoples who did not have this regard for sacred animals. We know the horror the Greeks had of being eaten by fishes or dogs instead of being favoured by the grace of fire.

Jacob Grimm is probably not far wrong in his assumption that warlike and nomad peoples incline to burning and agricultural peoples to simple burial. The attitude of the hunter and soldier to sun, fire, wood and field is entirely different from that of the tiller of the soil whose blessing comes from the ground and who year after year experiences its inexhaustible renewal of all life. Grimm may be equally right, though on less sure ground, when he says that we must suppose a cycle of changes in European forms of burial; that is to say, an original predominance of the simple burial in earth, which, because of some experiences or other, was succeeded by burning. There then followed a fresh, victorious attack by burial in earth, carried out by Christianity and the teaching of Mohammed. The Jews have always buried their dead, although there are traces of fire worship. Christ was buried and, following His example, the custom spread throughout the entire Occident. Like everything pagan, cremation seemed to Christianity to be idolatry and an outrage against the true God. This horror is still quite plain in the attitude of the Church to modern cremation. But it seems that in this disenchanted world the simple burial in earth has, for reasons of hygiene and economy, again reached the turning point.

Gaia, the goddess of death, from whom a number of gruesome and fabulous creatures spring, was named in

Homer immediately after Zeus when solemn oaths were taken; when Agamemnon gave Achilles Briseis back, he swore that he had not touched the maid—

> Witness thou first! Thou greatest power above;
> All-good, all-wise, and all-surveying Jove!
> And mother earth, and heaven's revolving light,
> And ye, fell furies of the realms of night,
> Who rule the dead, and horrid woes prepare
> For perjured kings, and all who falsely swear!
> The black ey'd maid inviolate removes,
> Pure and unconscious of my manly loves.

Here, as in the oath which Agamemnon swore when Paris and Menelaos wished to take the place of their people and fight a duel, the old goddess of the earth, the creative mother of everything, is called upon with the elements. Similarly Tellus, the might deity of growth, is repeatedly mentioned in the most solemn Roman oaths. A higher stratum of development leaves out the earth itself to make place for the goddess of the home and peaceful culture, Vesta. Countless passages from Roman historians show how much the cult of Vesta belonged to the prosperity of Rome. For that reason it was considered a terrible misfortune if the fire in the temple of Vesta went out. Then the Vestal who had been on watch that night was flayed by the High Priest. The Vestal who violated her oath and yielded to love was sacrificed, up to historical times, to the goddess of the earth. Apart from this practice, we know of only one instance of sacrifice by burial alive in Rome. This sacrificial rite was carried out in 216 B.C. on a Gallic man and woman and a Greek couple. The victims were put into an underground walled chamber. It was a time of national disaster, the battle of Cannæ had been fought and lost, and, apart from that, Vestals had been convicted of

91

immorality. "That room of stone built in the ground under the cattle market," says Livy, "had even formerly, quite contrary to the spirit of the Romans' reverence for the gods, received men as sacrifices."

In this year of disaster, two Vestals, Opimia and Floronia, were convicted of forbidden love and one was buried in the front of the Colline Gate, while the other committed suicide, and her lover was beaten to death by the Pontifex Maximus. Livy tells of a similar execution of a Vestal by burial at the Colline Gate, " on the right of the paved road in the Campus Sceleratus " in the year 419 A.U.C.

From Dionysius of Halicarnassus Mommsen has reconstructed the procedure more exactly. The guilty woman was stripped of her priestly insignia and to the sound of the customary lamentations carried on a bier to the grave—the grave consisted of a subterranean passage which, usually covered up, was only opened for these executions. In it a couch was made up and a loaf of bread and jugs of water, milk and oil were put in. While the Pontifex Maximus prayed, the condemned woman went down a ladder into the grave, whose opening was then covered up. No honouring of the grave was permitted.

Plutarch gives a similar but more detailed description. " If one lost her maiden honour, she was buried alive near the Colline Gate. There is there, still inside the city, a rise in the ground which stretches far out and in Latin is called ' agger.' Here a subterranean room is built, of small proportions and with an entrance from above. In it there is a complete couch, a burning light and a small quantity of the essentials of life, *i.e.*, bread, water in a jug, milk, oil and such things; in order, as it were, that they should not be guilty of giving a person consecrated to the most important religious offices over to death by starvation. The delinquent herself is placed in a sedan chair which is closely covered up and fastened with straps, so that not even her voice can be heard any longer. Thus she is carried over the Forum; everyone steps silently out of the way and in the silence of deepest mourning accompanies her. There is, indeed, no other spectacle so gruesome, nor a day of such grief as this day. When the chair reaches the place, the servants undo the straps, the Pontifex Maximus says some secret prayers, raises his hands to the gods and lets the deeply veiled woman step out and puts her on the ladder which leads down into the chamber. When she has climbed down, the ladder is withdrawn and the chamber covered up, and earth shovelled over it until the place is levelled up with the rest of the ground.

This is the punishment of Vestals who have abandoned the sacred honour of maidenhood.''

The first mention of burial alive among the Germans is found in Tacitus; it was practised in the case of cowards, weaklings and effeminate men. Should one be in doubt as to whether sinking a person in a moor or swamp belonged more to drowning or burial, the briars thrown over the criminal show its close connexion with burial alive. The Burgundian law speaks of sinking a person in wet filth. The condemned person was bound, thrown into a hole over which earth was thrown and trodden down. Burial alive was a woman's punishment, and sometimes the delinquent was given an air-tube in her mouth. In the Middle Ages the practice spread of driving a pointed stake of oak through the belly or heart and fixing the body with it. This fixing to the earth, exteriorly considered a mitigation, was a defence against the return of the dead, in the same way as criminals

93

were then also impaled. The heaped-up briars were also
a preventive of return, a hedge between this world and
the next. The stone placed on the corpse of ' the dishonourable woman ' was also to fix her down.

In the legal codes of the Middle Ages this punishment
gradually died out, but it is more or less regularly mentioned as a rare occurrence. In Villingen there is no
express mention of the punishment, but it may still
have been used, as it is on record that at Uberlingen
Margaretha Heiligin was impaled and buried alive and
then, to aggravate the punishment, was dug up again and
burned to ashes. In Nürnberg in 1513 there was a scene
at the burial of a girl alive, so gruesome that the
executioner refused to carry out any more sentences of
the kind, and drowning was introduced. Up to 1532
there is only one known case of burial alive in Frankfurt.
In Speyer the punishment is not mentioned. One case is
known in Bâle (1483), and it was used at Zurich, Lucerne
and Ensisheim. Osenbrüggen has collected statements on
burial alive from the legal codes of Augsburg, Ulm and
Strassburg, together with the old Swiss court usages of
Glarus and Schwyz. He gives us details from Zurich.
Ulrich Moser, who had outraged six little girls of
between four and nine years, was executed on 17th
August, 1465. He was stripped, laid on his back, bound
to four pegs in the ground, a stake was placed on his
navel and driven through his body into the ground,
and so was left to die. It is striking that the majority
of the executions mentioned took place in the second
half of the fifteenth century.

As in Roman sacerdotal law, the killing of Vestals
represented something intermediate between burial and
walling in and there is no lack of reports of execution
by means of the latter in Germany. Frankfurt

authorities twice mention ' walling in ' (1430). Grimm
mentions an occurrence in Zurich and several linguistic
fragments. In Bâle ' walling in ' was chiefly applied
to persons of noble blood, whose families asked for this
punishment instead of the death penalty or eternal
banishment from the city. It was a favour which spared
them the ignominy of a public execution and of being
touched by the executioner and was probably carried
out at night. Metzger mentions a single case of walling
in for sorcery from Bâle judicial praxis. According to
tradition, people to whom respect is due, such as monks,
nuns, wives of knights and girls of noble birth, were
always walled in. Legend says that the lords of the castle
had their daughters or adulterers immured. In the castle
at Haarburg a princess was walled in, and according to
one legend a robber baron in 1470 had a childhood's
friend of his wife's immured in Dobra Castle (Austria).

It is true that the immured was given a scanty supply
of food sufficient to last until he died of exhaustion or
cold. From this it is only a step to letting him starve
to death, a form of punishment which again approaches
hanging in chains. Hüllman tells of such an execution in
Augsburg in 1499. The victims were ecclesiastics. '' Four
were shut, bound hand and foot, into wooden cages which
hung from the Perlach Tower. After six days they died
of hunger and their bodies were buried on the Gallows
Hill by the hangman's servants.''

It is comparatively easy to connect burial alive, as a
criminal punishment, directly with its origin as a sacrifice. In expiatory sacrifice, especially among Germans
and Slavs, burial appears again and again.

Every new building, be it house or bridge, was a place
of vague perils which had to be exorcised and propitiated.
In Germanic tradition the first to cross a bridge or enter

a house will expiate his hazardous enterprise with death. Even in the Middle Ages when laying the foundation stones of castles, town walls, bridges and weirs, when building dykes, &c., children (sometimes even adults) were immured alive to give the building durability and prosperity; and in pulling down walls skeletons have often been found with and without coffins. We have already mentioned these sacrifices to buildings. Panzer tells of a typical legend of this kind from Bavaria: " When the castle of Vestenberg was built, the mason made a seat in the wall on which a child was put and walled up. The child wept, and, to quieten it, it was given a nice, red apple."

There are very many accounts of such human sacrifices, which, when they were to serve the stability of a building, were accomplished by burial. A child is supposed to have been buried in the embankment of the Jadebusen in order to make it strong. Other creatures, beside humans, were used as sacrifices; puppies, which were buried alive under the manger to keep the horses healthy; oxen, horses or a black hen. All Indo-Germanic peoples have a tendency towards such beliefs. In India ' the lord of the place ' lives in the ground, and must be propitiated if one wishes to build a new house. On the land dwells ' the lord of the fields ' to whom sacrifices are made when the ground is prepared for sowing.

Coins placed in foundation stones are a sacrifice to the spirit of the ground, as the bottle broken over the bow of a ship on the slipway is an offering to the spirit of the deep, to whom men were, and are, sacrificed by savage tribes.

The nearer the victim is to the one who benefits, the more effective is the sacrifice. Here the sacrificial suitability of the most guilty, the criminal, conflicts with that of the most innocent.

Similarly as with the punishment of burning, with burial alive there only remains for our consideration as the possible aim of the procedure, that of guarantee and deterrent, and if we clear away the rubble of the centuries, its original magical and religious stratum is clearly visible; the way in which the guilty Vestal priestess was given up to the powers of the earth admits of no other explanation. Into these beliefs flows a stream of Indo-Germanic conceptions. For them, burial, nailing down, keeping down with a thorn-barrier are more a magical defence against radically evil powers and ghostly substances. Even to-day a similar amalgamation of magical and expiatory effect can be seen in Germanic superstitions connected with burial. To the younger strata belong buried sacrifices which have an expiatory purpose. In Bohemia at the first sowing, the people go at night in a great procession with a naked girl and a completely black tom cat, round whose neck a lock has been hung, to the field, where a deep hole is dug and the cat buried alive; in other places in the spring a cat is buried under a tree in the garden or a field, so that the ' evil spirit ' shall not damage trees or fields. Other forms of burial of totally different character project from the uttermost depths of human spiritual life, the belief in magic, into the present time. In the burying of hair and nails with its striving after magical ends, there is a magical ' act of freeing oneself '; as in burying of warts, fever, toothache, gout, jaundice and every pain. This often touches the borders of incomprehensibility. But is this mixture of unreality and tremendous life-force really different from many things in penal law?

PUNISHMENT

Quartering

The hangman or executioner is, in many districts of Germany, called butcher or meat-carver, as in the Bible of 1483. This expression still persists in thieves' slang.

If we examine more closely the method of executing by quartering, which is still prescribed by the Carolina (Art. 124), we are struck by its conformity with the slaughtering of animals. The pictures of quartering which Fehr collected (especially the execution of Mathias Vulgo Windbeutel, from the Nürnberg German Museum) are no different from the everyday happenings in an abattoir.

It is not quite clear whether the bestial punishment of disembowelling constitutes the lowest stratum in the development of this punishment; it is still preserved in a drawing by the elder Lucas Cranach (1516). The bowels of the executed person were burned, like the guts of an animal. As well as being the punishment for high treason, disembowelling was the punishment usually prescribed by law for wanton damaging of trees; and we know how trees and thickets were venerated. If a person killed a tree by stripping off its bark, as much of his bowels was taken out of his body as sufficed to cover up the damaged place. As we have seen, it is still the popular custom in Germany and Slavonic east-coast countries to see something living and holy in trees and to make sacrifices to them. The lights in Xmas trees are a remnant of such a sacrifice.

There were several cases of quartering in the district of Villingen during the fifteenth and sixteenth centuries. There is a description of such an execution in Uberlingen. Here, already humanized, it is preceded by decapitation, for, according to the old formula, two parts

98

were to be made of the criminal, and in such a way that the head was the smaller. Then his body was opened up, his bowels taken out and buried. Finally, the trunk was divided into four which were to be stuck up on different parts of the gallows. The head could be stuck up on a nail.

Another somewhat different procedure was prescribed by the Swiss Freien-Aemter Landgerichtsordnungen for traitors to their country. To begin with, their treacherous hearts together with all their bowels shall be cut from their bodies; then follows beheadal and quartering. In one case, which occurred in Lausanne and which is established by Osenbrüggen, a servant who had murdered his master, the bishop, was quartered after his kidneys —as seat of his wicked disposition—had been torn from his body with red-hot pincers.

In Bâle the old sacrificial axe was produced at quarterings; the punishment was inflicted by the executioner with the help of the gravediggers, with axe and knife, and as a general rule on a living body. Executions of this kind are known in Rheinfelden and several in Bâle. In the great trading city of Frankfurt, which early became cultured, it was only the corpse which was quartered. Rau found only three cases up to the year 1532, and always in conjunction with beheadal. The remains were fastened on to wheels, the wheels set up on the city walls where they were visible from every direction.

Of historical interest are the executions of Balthazar Gérard, murderer of the Prince of Orange, and of the Franconian knight, Wilhelm von Grumbach. The former was tortured for two days till he died. On the first day he was flayed and rubbed over with salt, and needles were stuck into his fingers. On the next day his flesh was torn with red-hot pincers; his body was opened up and his heart cut out and put in his hand, where it was stabbed, to the words, " The treacherous murderer of his own master must rightly get such a terrible reward." Then he was quartered and his quarters set up in different places.

A terrible picture of a terrible time was the execution of Grumbach at Gotha in 1567. He was stripped, laid on his back and bound or nailed down; then his heart was cut from his body and thrown in his face by the hangman with the words, " See, Grumbach, your false heart." Then followed quartering. The whole procedure reminds one of the rape murders committed by madmen who hang the sexual organs of their victim on the surrounding trees.

The rôle of entrails in Greek and Roman cults is well known. In German superstition the entrails of animals are a sure defence against magic. The custom of quartering goes right back to prehistoric times; its occurrence in the Middle Ages is only fitful. It is not the skinning and cutting up of the body that is the chief thing, but the fact that a way is forced to the last stronghold of all life, the heart. Thus magical elements are mixed with later sacrificial rites and we can hear even to-day, when people are excited by some crime, proposals of exemplary punishment, which closely resemble the old forms of destruction.

Tearing asunder by means of horses seems to be older than quartering with axe and knife. Grimm puts forward a great deal of evidence in support of this. The last recorded sentence of the kind was passed on Damiens for the attempted murder of Louis XV of France in 1757, but although four powerful horses were employed they failed to dismember him.

People were also dragged to death by horses or oxen; the criminal being bound to the tail of the animal which was as wild as possible and the animal then spurred or goaded on. We come across this again as a severer form of the penalties of breaking on the wheel or quartering. The condemned person was bound on an ox-hide or a kind of sledge and pulled by a horse to the place of execution. According to the Zurich Blutgerichtsordnung's formula, the executioner was commanded to bind the condemned person on his back to a board, bind his feet to a horse's tail and drag him thus to the place of execution. Rau mentions a Frankfurt entry where dragging and quartering are entered together in the account books. In Frankfurt only murderers were condemned to be dragged to the place of execution. Achilles dragged the body of Hector round the walls of Troy and the ashes of Hus were dragged to the Rhine and thrown into the water.

The significance of dragging is obscure, but I suggest this explanation. In the Iliad, Achilles bewails his dead friend, '' Who lies in my tent, turned to the door, hacked by the pointed lances.''

It is the position of the dead man which is meant, his feet pointing to the way out. There are to-day still current countless superstitious practices to hinder the return of the dead or to make him lose his way should he wish to creep back. At Indian burials a branch from a tree is bound to the feet of the corpse to wipe out its footprints. The road back is disguised for dangerous spirits, those of murderers in the Germanic Middle Ages. There is perhaps a similar idea at the back of the old custom of dragging the corpse. The dead person would be unable to recognize his footprints in the track of the ox-hide or plank and would stay away.

101

PUNISHMENT

Precipitation

While in Greek mythology women often committed suicide by hanging themselves, for men the heroic way of voluntary departure from life was to jump from a height. Diodorus emphasizes the fact that when the old Ægeus saw a ship with black sails steering towards Attica he ended his life by a deed " which was worthy of a hero " in throwing himself down from the citadel. The manly Sappho being, according to the story, disappointed in her love for Phaon, jumped into the sea from the Leucadian cliffs.

Ehrenberg has drawn attention to the name of Themiscyra, which occurs in the legend of Theseus. This city, the white rock of Themis, is handed over to Theseus by the Amazon Antiope, who has fallen violently in love with him. Hippolytus is their son. According to Ehrenberg, the white rock plays a double part in Greek religious ideology. The entrance to the underworld is supposed to be at the white rocks, and Homer (Odyssey, xxiv, 11) places them on the road of the dead suitor to the underworld. But, further, an ancient ritual of purification is connected with the white rocks; to jump from the rocks expiates blood guilt. This is, according to Ehrenberg, a rite frequently connected with Apollo cults and we can understand it as such when Ovid on several occasions mentions Apollo. The Naiad who appeared to Sappho in a dream speaks of Phœbus, who from the cliffs looks over the sea to the horizon. It is consistent with this that Deucalion and his wife, on being saved from the flood, called upon ' the powers of the mountains ' and Themis, who was now in possession of the Delphic oracle. Themis, however, one of the Titans, daughter of Uranos, and the goddess of the earth, is closely connected with the gates of the deep and the earth oracle. It is perhaps easiest for us to connect a curious manner of death and Greek polytheism, if we remember that the gods were ' stratified ' in Delphi. There one imagined the old earth spirit Python dwelling deep down like an evil dragon; and only after him came Apollo. As he began to dominate in the ideas of the Greeks, the spirit of the depths, whose breath rose in a cold current of air from a split in the mountain, died, and Apollo's sanctuary was raised on the grave of him whom he had defeated. The powers of chaos, of the unclean and wicked, were broken by the beneficial and expiatory power of the god of light.

The expiatory and voluntary leap from cliffs and the expiatory forcible precipitation of a criminal is, according to this, probably a continuation of sacrificial customs which had a clear meaning with the elder of the deities of the earth. The rock took the place of the cleft in the earth, under which the threatening brood of the depths lay; here sacrifices were made in countries where earthquakes and volcanic upheavals were frequent.

It is possible that the victory of Apollo and his milder religion coincided with a period of weakening telluric activity. The dive into the sea from the cliffs found in Poseidon, the god of the sea, the successor of pythonic powers, the earth shaker. Custom and law developed from persistent surrender to the threatening powers of the underworld. Themis is the daughter of Gaea, of the Earth and Uranos.

Greek mythology is full of tales of penal precipitations. Tantalus is cast down from heaven to the evil ones and condemned to eternal torment, because he had betrayed the secrets of the gods. Hermes throws Argus from the cliff, after cutting off his head with a scimitar. Hercules throws Iphitus down from the top of the tower, and being smitten with madness for this murder, he consults Apollo as to how he may be cured. He sells himself to Omphale as a slave and gives the money as compensation to Iphitus' sons; this is perhaps the first suggestion of redemption from the blood-penalty by means of blood-money. This blood-money is earned by an act of self-punishment—in this case the hero abasing himself to become the slave and servant of a woman. Dædalus, being jealous of Talus's inventive genius, throws him down from the citadel. We must also imagine how Phæthon dived into the sea from the steep paths of heaven on which the tracks of his wheels can still clearly be recognized.

Of older origin are those forms of downfalls, where one fell from heaven or the earth into Tartarus, into the bowels of the earth; even Saturn is thrown down with the Titans into the depths, and Gæa is angry because Uranos had thrown her first children into Tartarus.

Here we come across that very old idea of the Greek religions which Rhode has treated in a fine chapter on cave-gods and those swallowed up by mountains. Amphiarus before whom the earth opened, cleft by a bolt from Zeus, was one of those who made a journey into the bowels of the earth to hell. He drove down with his wagon and horses and continued to live inside the earth. Likewise in Bœotia immortal Trophonius lives in a cave. Caineus drove into the bowels of the earth. Althemenes disappeared into a crater on Rhodes. All those who were thus swallowed up live separated by a thin layer of earth from man whose prayers can reach them. They are joined by Erechteus, born of the earth, who lives in the ancient sanctuary of the Acropolis; and Hyacinthus who is buried at Amyclæ and to whom the Spartans every year sent sacrifices. Here again an old demon of the earth sits under the ground of the temple, to whom the prayers and offerings of men descend; inextinguishable in man's memory, although new and lighter gods have pushed aside the old, dark figures.

The Mediterranean peoples, to whom crevasses, waters and lakes from which mephitic mists rise, are commonplace, saw the combination of fire and water, the forces of the deep and of life. They swore their most sacred oaths at such spots where the elements mingled. Phæthon's fall was used " to explain the miracle of a spring from which hot or mephitic vapours rose, and which was called ' Eridanos,' the matutinal," because of the fire-demon who was thought to continue active in it.

Everywhere in Greece where a white rock marks an entrance to Hades there are hallowed sanctuaries. When the community lies under blood-guilt, the guilt is put on to an individual who is thrown from the cliff, an expiatory sacrifice being made of him. Thus there is certain proof of the sacrificial character of precipitation from rocks in Greece. A weakened form of this expiatory sacrifice was that the person consulting the oracle descended into a cleft in the ground and then carried out other expiations as advised by the deity.

Precipitation from a rock belongs, as a criminal punishment, to Roman law. On the south side of the Capitol, which rose some fifty metres above the river, there must have been a steep cliff. This was the Tarpeian Rock, named after Tarpeia, who treacherously opened the Citadel to the Sabines, who showed their opinion of her by piling their shields upon her so that she died. She is said to have been buried near the spot. At one time there had been the Lacus Curtius near the

105

Forum, but in the course of time it was diverted. Later, however, there occurred a sudden sinking and an abyss was formed into whose depths a sacrifice was thrown. Then on the spot of the old mountain fissure an altar was erected from which there was probably an opening into the depths. Livy himself tells, with a certain amount of disbelief, of a human sacrifice which removed a danger to the city of Rome. "In this very year," he writes, "either an earthquake or some tremendous force is supposed to have riven a cleft of immeasurable depth in more or less the middle of the market place; and all the earth which the people brought and shovelled in could not fill this abyss. Then the story goes that Marcus Curtius, a youth who had distinguished himself in the war, raising his eyes to the temples of the immortal gods, which rose steep above the market place, and to the Capitol, and now folding his arms in prayer, now stretching them to the heavens or to the gods of the dead in the wide opening in the earth, consecrated himself a sacrifice and in full armour, on his horse, which he had decked out as finely as possible, leaped into the abyss. A crowd of men and women threw gifts and fruit after him and from this the Curtian lake got its name."

It is not certain whether the worship of deities of the underworld which, in historical times, had in Rome taken on milder forms, was derived from the religion of the Etruscans. The throwing of sacrifices into crevasses could easily have come to them from this country of large crater lakes and telluric unrest, which sought to defend itself from earthquakes and the deities of lightning by worshipping them and which was strongly influenced by the Greeks.

As a legal institution precipitation from the Tarpeian Rock exhibits two clearly distinguishable forms, one of which, executed by the injured, goes back to the earliest times. This, we know, occurred in the case of two infringements of the Law of the Twelve Tables—*furtum manifestum* by a slave stealing and perjury. The sacredness of an oath was a worthy part of pious antiquity. At first an oath had to be taken in the open air, so that the perjurer should be struck down by Zeus's lightning before the false oath had passed his lips. If a general had not fulfilled the promises given to the enemy, he was handed over to them together with his chief officers, naked and with their hands bound, that is to say, prepared like religious sacrifices. The curse of perjury was to fall on their heads alone, likewise the anger of the disappointed enemy. In taking an oath, we always find among the gods called upon, as well as Zeus, the gods of the underworld, or, connected with them, the bones of one's mother or her ashes. In ancient Rome, Numa, according to the legend, dedicated a temple and a feast day to himself and also a temple to Vesta, the goddess of the earth. We cannot doubt that there is a connexion between the punishment of the Vestal who broke her oath and the punishment of the perjurer, who was thrown into a crevasse; that is to say, each was delivered up to the earth.

As well as in cases of execution by the injured party, this precipitation from the rock was used for executions by the tribunes and many summary measures of the patrician magistrates; above all, during riots this impressive method of execution was used to prevent rebellion. Man's part in the execution was lessened in that it was confined to arrest and forcible transport to the place whence the person was to be thrown. After which the force of gravity became the instrument of killing. An aggravation of the punishment was the lack of regular burial, for the bodies fell into the river, or were thrown into it after execution.

When the tribunes threw Manlius from the Tarpeian Rock, there woke in the people, as Livy says, a longing for him. Moreover, a pestilence broke out and the anger of the gods was traced to this summary execution. " The Capitol is profaned by the blood of its saviour and for the gods, the execution of the man who had torn their temple from the enemies' hands, which was made practically an exhibition, was an abomination." Here religious ideas, although of negative tendency, still clearly came into play. The procedure in throwing a person from the rock is made plain in a passage from Plutarch. " Then the most daring of the people's tribunes Sicinnius conferred a moment or two with his colleagues and then made public the announcement that Marcius (Coriolanus) was condemned by the tribunes to death. At the same time he ordered the ædiles to take him to the citadel and to have him thrown immediately into the abyss below. So a short conference of a moment or two was sufficient and the sentence was executed without delay. But as the populace assumed a threatening attitude, the friends and acquaintances of the tribunes induced them " to remove from the punishment its quite unusual and doubtful character, by leaving it to the people to vote on his fate, instead of having him killed forcibly and without a preliminary trial." Thus the summary procedure is diverted into the customary procedure.

Deserters, too, were thrown from the rock. When the consuls Q. Fabius and M. Marcellus took a number of cities by storm, 370 deserters fell into their hands. To make an example of them, the consuls sent them to Rome where they were flogged in the Forum and then thrown from the Tarpeian Rock.

EVOLUTION OF PUNISHMENT

The old legendary procedure did not always make the impression expected of it. It is after Cæsar's death . . . " Thereupon the people rushed upon Cæsar's body which some wanted to take to the Capitol and burn there, while others wished to burn it in the Curia itself, where he was murdered. Being prevented from doing this by the soldiers, because they could easily have burned down the theatre and the temple with it, they built up the funeral pyre in the market place itself and burned it. But even so many buildings in the neighbourhood would have gone up in smoke if the soldiers had not prevented it and the consuls had not thrown some of the wildest from the Tarpeian Rock. Even this did not quieten the crowds, and they rushed to the homes of the murderers and in their fury killed, among others, the tribune of the people, Helvius Cinna, who had not only not taken part in the conspiracy, but had been Cæsar's most faithful adherent.

Other provocative delicts besides were punished with precipitation from the rock. Under Tiberius sorcerers and astrologers were driven out of Italy; one of them, L. Pituanius, was thrown from the Tarpeian Rock. For a false accuser the people demanded the punishment of a great criminal, that is to say, either that he should be thrown from the Tarpeian Rock or drowned in a sack. And, finally, a very rich man, the greatest landed proprietor in Spain, was thrown from the Rock, on a charge of incest with his daughter that had been trumped up so that, by inspiring feelings of disgust in the people, the true character of the affair—a judicial robbery with murder—might pass unnoticed.

As we get more remote from the earthquake countries of Greece and Italy, cases of precipitation as a death penalty grow fewer and fewer. It is only in a third

Mediterranean country—Spain—that throwing from a rock has since ancient times been the principal death penalty, and a Greek poet tells of a similar custom on the steep coast of Crimea. The custom lost its mechanical basis as the old custom of building cities on inaccessible rocks decreased with the rise of culture and the fearful worship of the powers of the underworld gave way to milder religious conceptions.

Amira has been unable to find any trace of the independent death penalty of precipitation from a rock in Germanic legal papers, except in the English. In old Germanic and Scandinavian law this punishment appears sporadically. Amira and Grimm mention, too, the punishment of ' falling ' localized to Bavaria; the condemned person with bound eyes is thrown on a plank into a hole or well. Vivid is the recollection of criminals thrown down in Iceland and the Faroes; here, too, certain cliffs were used as places of execution. When Iceland went over to Christianity in the year 1000, the Christians reproached the pagan country people that their worship with sacrifices was bound up with abominations: '' The heathens sacrifice the worst people and throw them over rocks and cliffs.'' In this reproach the intimate interwovenness of sacrificial usage and criminal punishment is expressed. The choice of definite cliffs in England, Iceland and the Faroes also points to the close connexion between place of worship and place of execution.

Legend, however, has preserved legal customs which are otherwise lost to memory. '' Criminals were thrown down from a jutting rock, or they had themselves to jump down. Such rocks were the Isle of the Dead at Zoothen, the Lasterberg at Paska, &c. In Austria, ' The Rose Garden ' is a ledge of rock on the Castle of Aggstein, well known as a death rock. The lords of the castle gave the prisoners the choice of starving on the rock or of throwing themselves down into the deep Danube. Some romantic legends have been handed down about this.

There are scattered over Germany many ' Devil's Pulpits,' whose significance has not been explained. Wuttke supposes them to have been ancient places of worship.

The way in which some sagas correspond with the Greek legends of the underworld is striking. Panzer relates the following about the ' Devil's Church ' in Middle Franconia. " . . . Following this wild ravine to its beginning, one reaches the Devil's Church, a mound with a shaft hewn out of the rock, leading straight down." The figure of the devil has taken the place of the old figures of gods and giants. It was not only the Cyclopes who coveted human flesh, and human flesh can put the irascible cragsmen in a forgiving mood; Grimm has introduced a giant from Indian mythology; a mis-shapen, red-bearded cannibal. The Germanic giants have already divested themselves of this fearsome trait; and the fact that there are only faint traces of a worship with sacrifices to be found, may be connected with this.

However, that which has disappeared from memory persists with tremendous tenacity in man's emotional life and wakes to new life at certain moments of excitement. The *Fenstersturz* in Prague (23rd May, 1615) and the revolutionary executions in the old Roman city of Nimes in 1791, are historical examples of this.

The Curse

If we disregard its magical beginnings, the sacerdotal origin of the death penalty is the original structure in the tectonic of conceptions which for thousands of years have piled one on top of the other. Supernatural and over-ruling powers which inscrutably dominate the life of poor and fearful man, are disposed to clemency by the surrender of the cause of their anger. To care for the guilty was an outrage and theft from the deity, and might not be considered for one instant by those whom it imperilled.

The idea of sacrifice receded, but a rational view of punishment was slow to emerge. We are always apt to forget that for the majority of people man's life still consists of two halves, an existence on earth and an imagined existence as a ghost in another sphere. Not much is gained by removing the guilty person from this life, for death merely transfers him to a higher, unassailable and dangerous form of existence, into which he takes with him his wickedness, to say nothing of the desire for revenge on his tormentors. This malign inquietude affects, not only those who have been executed, but all who have died a violent death by hunger, murder or suicide. In general the period of haunting is regarded as a period of transition at the end of which there is either complete redemption or eternal damnation.

With the vague recollections of the sacrificial character of the punishment are now mixed attempts to chain up the vagrant dead and prevent their returning in anger, and also the destruction of the living. Without this idea, which, stronger even than fear of the living, dominated those who inflicted punishment, certain forms of punishment which are directed neither against man's life, nor his susceptibility to pain, are incomprehensible, even absurd. They are measures against an autonomous, restless, indeed, ' criminal ' impulse of the soul, which is attached to the life on earth. As the soul allows itself

112

to be adjured and summoned, certain curtailments, with which we have become acquainted, have the power to check or completely to hinder its free mobility; and here expedients of penal law encroach on spheres which were created only by the hopes and fears of religious belief.

So defence against the haunting dead stands beside defence against the angry deity and breaks out like an ulcer from man's thoughts in an inventive technique of punishment; even the modern punishments with a definite aim, still carry with them much too much of this inheritance.

A closely connected association between the power of the gods and man's will appears in the curse as a means of punishment which, confined to the narrow scope of perjury, has only a shadowy existence on the borders of modern justice. In olden days a powerful, one could practically say etiolated, life was given to curses.

Psychologically, prayers and curses are not to be differentiated. Where faith instils prayer with the magic power of compelling the deity to descend from his cloudy heights and lend the help, defence and blessing of his presence, there, too, the punitive intervention of the gods must be capable of being compelled by the magic of ardent words. By his prayers Elijah brought drought and God's lightning from heaven and snatched from God the soul of the child which he had already taken to Himself.

In order to be able to approach the deity with the concentrated ardour of the will, in many religions a pause for reflexion was made before and after prayer, as is done when great physical exertion is called for.

The gifts of the gods for which one stretched out one's hands and which one endeavoured to win by means of magical formulæ, could take forms of assistance other than health, virtue or earthly happiness; they might be vengeance on an enemy, whom one's curses bound up with the breach of the moral code and the watchfulness of the guardian deity. Three stages in the development of the curse are to be noted. There was, first, the curse to avenge something that had happened; then came the curse to ward off a threatened disaster; and the third and final stage is self-execration, for the purpose of guaranteeing the performance of an action or attesting the truth of a statement; here we reach the form in which cursing survives as part of modern legal procedure —the last relic of an ancient faith.

In Mosaic law the death penalty is prescribed for cursing as a form of [attempted] murder, though only in one case. " He that curseth his father or his mother, shall surely be put to death." " His blood be upon him, that he cursed his father or mother." In an acrimonious argument with the Pharisees, Christ refers to this statement in the Law. Moses would hardly have made so severe a law, if he had not credited the spoken word with the actual power of hurting, like a stone or arrow. Thus among the Jews it was strictly forbidden to curse the authorities and when King David pardoned Shimei, in spite of his having cursed him, we see that Solomon condemned his father's mildness, his forgiveness of the curse and the thrown stone, and took the first opportunity that offered, when Shimei broke his open arrest, to have him executed. The superhuman might of the will and of its most threatening form of expression, the word, has been acknowledged by Indians and Greeks as well as Romans, in that magic formulæ were reckoned among methods of poisoning, for which the penalty was death. A similar power was credited to curses, and above all to curses upon one's father, which the gods themselves employed.

Grimm has given a good description of the power of curses: " Songs and tunes have the power to do the greatest things, they can kill, wake from death and secure one against it; heal and make sick; bind up wounds and stop bleeding; relieve pain; induce sleep; put out fire; abate storms and the sea; send rain and hail; burst bands and tear chains asunder; pull back bolts; open and close mountains; reveal treasure; loosen or close the ends of rings; make weapons strong or weak; dull swords; tie knots; strip the bark from trees; ruin seed; summon or banish evil spirits; tie up thieves . . ."

In superstition the omnipotence of the deity is compelled by man's will as in the criminal procedure and religious rites of the old peoples. As Wuttke says: " the single man with his fortuitous, often sinful, will makes himself governor of the world's moral order; *his* will shall be done in good and evil; as an expression of love, fear and hate."

Thus in curses upon others or oneself and in the oath, we see the forces of heaven tied to man's words and thoughts, sunk to an earthly level and serving man's laws and regulations. The sacred character of punishment appears in its purest form in the curse, man's peace, the balance of moral order and the execution of punishment are governed by magic formulæ which suppose a power of control dominating the gods and which the gods themselves use in their struggles with each other.

According to the laws of Zug, verbal injuries were not only the reproaching of one with actions and facts, but also the wishing of evil, like ' the devil take you.' Even Feuerbach considers that form of curse, which wishes that evil may come to another from the deity, as a crime against morality; but the fear of harmful effect has faded to a ' degradation of worthy objects ' or is hidden behind it. The curses of the weak (the dying, pregnant woman, and the dead) pass as being specially effective; this union of the defenceless with supernatural powers thus equalizes the injustice of real life. Thus curses belong to the mechanisms of faith, which man has made in order to establish confidence and hope for himself on a sentient and ethically founded issue of events. The ideas will not disappear, because they belong to the spiritual self-defence and will-to-live of those that labour and are heavy laden.

CHAPTER III

THE MENTAL CLASSIFICATION OF PUNISHMENT

1. IMPERATIVE THEORIES

Vengeance was exacted, men were outlawed, weregeld was given and taken, and public punishment decreed, all under the ruling force of custom, without any inquiry into their origin. The exploration of the character, purpose and legal basis of punishment (and with it the criticism of the prevailing penal praxis) belongs only to a later stage in mankind's development. The most primitive form of finding a legal argument for punishment is to say that it is derived from a divine will.

Divine Commandment

Machiavelli has acutely hinted at the connexion between belief in a deity and political life. This connexion between things divine and human legislation was implicitly accepted for thousands of years and one may say that it still persists in the emotional life of the masses. Little was changed when the dynasties of the gods fell. After a short period of confusion the will of the old gods was imperceptibly replaced by the commandments of the new deity.

Everything considered, it would appear that crime establishes relations only between the State, as holder of the power to punish, and the perpetrator. The injured person is completely forced into the background and only plays the part of provider of proof. The State, however,

117

has not always been the autonomous and secularized combination for the struggle for existence which we know to-day. It once was, and by many people still is, regarded only as the means of fulfilling missions which one calls 'higher' because they lie beyond the bare sociological function of the human state. This union with ultra-political powers, this subordination to a further 'higher' sphere of purpose draws punishment into another plane in respect of its purpose. If the State's ideal is a divine order and nothing more, the will of the deity stamped out into social forms, then crime is an offence against the duties of subordination; a refusal of obedience, mutiny and revolt. According to this belief, man is linked to God by faith, and the link must not be broken. Hence apostasy is a crime, an outrage, like taking leave without permission or desertion. Here there are still strong features of the characterization of a deity, which man has made in his own image. Neglect irritates, and reverence is rewarded with prosperity. He who gives to God any shape at all, can only do so by using human features, enlarging them and perfecting them as far as his own gift for moral gilding allows. Thus the deity is omniscient and omnipotent, but it allows man to get into fault, allows him to commit crimes and then demands atonement for its broken commandment.

Thus punishment can have actually no purpose for God's justice. As there is no question of purpose, the injured autocracy of God does not allow the king to practise clemency. The procedure of the Inquisition is for the same reason as that which Stahl details, quite harmonious with the Christian state. The accused is in a position of subjection to the prosecuting authorities. He thus owes every obedience, he must allow himself to be used as a means of reaching the objective truth and the administrators of justice must use him for this, because he is one of the best, very often the best, means of doing it. So he must be questioned, confronted with reasons for suspecting him and forced to support his version with positive details; so that, should he be unable to do this with conviction, suspicion is piled up against him—the real Inquisition.

Thus the threads of theocratic ideas reach deep down into the procedure against the accused and determine the measure of his rights while at the same time putting upon him the duty of clearing himself.

The religious teaching of the Israelites was at once their constitution and their penal law; the laws of Manu determined not only the punishment of the criminal in this world, but also fixed exactly the future punishments which awaited him in the other world, and even the punishments he would suffer should he return to the earth in the course of the transmigration of his soul. Not long ago the Koran was still the Mohammedans' Catechism and at the same time his penal code. The philosophy of law that Stahl expounded a hundred years ago is not now presented in the same nakedness, severity and one-sidedness; but although it is no longer bluntly stated that the state is of dual nature as the intermediate step between the realm of nature and the kingdom of God, one can still find among the theologians who express opinions on the problem of punishment, the conception of crime as revolt against a constitution of the world determined by a divine power. There exists, it is said, an " ethical causal nexus between man's moral behaviour and condition.'' Nature's private revenge on immoral actions corresponds to the punishment of crime.

The fact that the causal nexus between deed and consequence, if such there be, shows deplorable interruptions,

119

is disposed of by saying that God's ways are inscrutable and in any case the actual balancing of accounts will take place in another world.

The consideration of punishment from the religious point of view has important practical consequences. By dividing the sphere of reward and punishment into this world and the next, it is not only easier to explain the thesis that " on the strength of a metaphysical justness the reward is already contained in the practice of morality, as is punishment in immoral behaviour," but it is also made possible to add subordinate aims to the purely vindictive element of punishment, of which that of deterrence belongs to this world, that of reform to the other world. This curious association appears in the death penalty. Final physical destruction loses its horror for the believer, because the dying person's repentance is only the transition to an existence where he is surrounded with mercy and forgiveness. The penitent criminal stands purified in the other world. While he breathed, he was still a horrible warning, but in heaven, as one who has reformed, he shares in every bliss.

Out of this belief grows quite naturally an entirely different idea of criminal punishment. Earthly pain becomes a sensible, but passing evil. Destruction at the executioner's hand or through the consuming influences of the convict prison is stripped of all finality. Death is divested of all real deadliness and becomes a phase of transition into a more beautiful sphere of life.

Thus for the believer there are atoning and mitigating elements in the vindictive character of punishment which are refused the unbeliever. The modern State is faced with the question whether it can justify the use in a very earthly manner—namely, punishing a person—of conceptions in which future forgiveness and alleviations do not occur with anything like the certainty of earthly aggravation. For the State cannot, of course, see into the darkness of the other world, but it has become its business to be in every act of punishment a pattern of action, the broadcaster of powerful suggestions to millions of witnesses, sympathizers, persons positively or negatively excited, intimidated or incited to imitation. This earthly duty concerns it more closely than a consideration which comes within the sphere of faith.

At any rate, the other view, in the times which belonged to it, did not bring man any blessing. The judge who discharged his punitive duties by order of the deity, could only command that short period of the long-drawn-out event of punishment which was to be unfolded on earth. He could only allay the enmity of the indignant deity by severity of punishment, without being allowed to interfere in its later function of pardoning, which lay in the darkness of the other world. Because of this the doctrine of punishment as God's will led to that absolute form of justice, whose terrible climax is shown in the late Middle Ages and Renaissance, and whose traces more humane times have not even yet been able completely to remove from our penal code and ideas of punishment.

The " ethical causal nexus between man's moral behaviour and condition " of which the theologian spoke is an idea which is actually anterior to the appearance of clear ideas of God. " Just as diseases and similar destructive powers are thought of now as more constant, now as airy, transient substances, which can be washed away with water, burned up by fire, banished by magically powerful amulets or removed in many other ways, so too is sin (' enas ' as well as ' agas ') imagined," observes Oldenberg. But to whomever sin adheres, it evokes for him sickness or death; madness, too, can result from the " sin which comes from the gods; the substance of sin adhering to the sun, causes its darkening."

It was not till a further step in its development had been reached that the transgressed commandment of God was interposed between guilt and punishment. The guilt bacillus no longer drags the infected person down like a deadly and also infectious fever; the gods now persecute the sin and the sinner until he freed himself from their anger with his entreaties and gifts.

If one sees the essence of punishment as the atonement of a servant for failure to carry out a binding command, then the carrying out of such penal procedure, on a religious basis, depends on the contents of the precepts handed down to us as divine commandments. The great difficulty lies in the fact that the religious requisitions of, for example, the Old Testament, are cut to the measure of entirely different ethical conditions, of an entirely different climate, of a thinly populated agrarian highland country and a civilization which existed thousands of year ago. But as the law or a legal system founded on religion cannot put life in a strait-jacket, but develops out of the river of life, being at the same time fruit and seed, then the reduction of penal law to a divine commandment would only be conceivable on the supposition that the deity from time to time revised his will, making it elastic, like everything that lives and endures. The impressive power of the doctrine of divine command-ment lies, however, just in its incomprehensibility, its absolute tranquillity. Thus this principle is inappli-cable to a jurisprudence which has to do with this world.

The doctrine of divine right, which still has its cham-pions, has not only influenced the conception of the character of punishment itself, but must also have made a very deep impression on the erection of punishable actions and their valuation. Those offences, which were thought most to anger God, were considered the most terrible atrocities. At their head stand religious ' delicts,' treasonable attacks on God's state. Even in 1774 Klapproth wished blasphemy to be considered as the worst crime. He proposed cutting out the tongue, or whatever member should be involved in the blasphemy, burning the member before the perpetrator's eyes; beheading, burning the corpse and scattering the ashes. Offences against morality followed religious delicts as most serious offences against the divine commandment, the precepts of the Old Testament and the ordering of the world desired by God.

Grotius, in the first third of the seventeenth century, was the first to make a breach in this gloomy heresy. According to him, God has implanted social talents in man and sent him out into the world to use them. He was followed by Thomasius who was the first to dispute the Bible's character of a binding legal rule. Just as the physician watches over the health of the body, so should the prince watch over the State's moral ailments and combat them.

Over and over again Grotius used that frightening and, at that time, unheard-of word ' Interest ' (' *utilitas* '); he taught not to pay attention in punishing to what had happened, but to the future result of the treatment. Reprisals which clung only to the past he called purposeless self-gratification (*triumphum et gloriam animi*); punishment by reprisal he called no legal punishment but a hostile act (*pœna non est, sed factum hostile*). Thomasius preached prevention as the State's first duty. They were the forerunners of the age of enlightenment

to which all progress in science pure and applied is
due. Even in penal law that brilliant age has pushed
far past the frontiers behind which we are to-day again
beginning to withdraw, weary of so many marks of
decay.

Judicial Reprisal

As contemplative faith began to decline, the deity was
replaced by an impersonal abstract, called justice or the
ethical idea, and the theories of judicial reprisal, which
Kant and Hegel have widely propagated, were conceived. From the theological beginnings of penal law,
Kant took the imperative relationship between punisher
and punished: " Penal law is the right of the commander
against the subdued, the right to inflict a punishment
on him because of an offence. Kant draws a wide distinction between penal law and all considerations of
usefulness, " the sinuosities of the endaemonism," with
which he most probably alludes to the English philo-
sopher Bentham. Kant's ' justice ' of punishment has
nothing to do with the expediency of punishment, which
we would to-day call penology. " Even if a community
of citizens dissolves with the consent of every member
(e.g., the inhabitants of an island decide to separate and
spread all over the world), they must first execute the
last murderer in the prison, so that everyone gets what is
his due according to his deeds, and so that the people,
not having insisted on this punishment, should not be
under the blood-guilt; because they can be regarded as
accessories to this public violation of justice."

The use and idea of the word ' blood-guilt ' show that
even a mind so well trained in philosophy as Kant's lost
itself in atavistic emotional impulses as soon as it had
to do with matters of penal law. The age-old solution
of reprisal, the lex talionis, corresponded to his absolute

point of view. With this he arrived at absurd results; insults should be punished by the offender having to apologize or perhaps even by having to kiss the offended person's hand; rape and homosexuality with castration, sodomy with a kind of outlawry, &c. In cases of murder, reprisal unconditionally demanded the death penalty, because only death is equal to death.

Heinz says that Kant's services in deepening the idea of punishment and penal law can scarcely be valued too highly. " They consist in the apprehension and carrying through of the theorem that punishment cannot be justified by pure utility." But evolution has rather admitted the rightness of Bentham's saying, which Kant reproached with being a *raison fantastique*. It is impossible to combine an effective penal law with a Kantian moral penal code. So we must decide on a penal law based on the ordinary human requirement that it should fulfil the purpose for which it exists.

But before we leave absolute theories, we will take an example to illustrate how pure introspection and speculative fury lead the student of penal law astray. Köstlin. in a work which he calls " New Revision of the Fundamental Principles of Criminal Law," writes with all the bombast and deep mental confusion of his time: " Because the removal of an injury must appear as negation implanted in it, even as injury of the injurer, so must it, as external act, bear the same exactitude in kind and size, it must according to the principle of equal measure of worth be counter-retaliation of constraint by constraint."

Köstlin is the author of the phrase " . . . like the conception of freedom, the conception of the soul too everywhere is first realized as negativity against nature." It is obviously impossible either to found a doctrine of punishment, or to cope with crime in any practical way in so unnatural a spirit. It is the degradation of pure intellect to absolute nonsense.

2. THEORIES OF PURPOSE

The General Purpose of Penal Law

Sigerist has very pointedly said that we speak of sickness as of a living creature. But sickness does not exist apart from the sick person. There are only sick people and for that reason the course of sickness does not run irregularly, inaccessible to investigation and treatment, but it is bound to the same bodily substratum as physiological functions. The same symptoms of sickness appear in the most different people, because the biological mechanisms, and, as one might say, the releasing forces are the same.

Just as in primitive medicine there were originally three elements—empirical, magical and religious—so in criminal law, with this difference that in criminal law the empirical element has not yet wholly supplanted its rivals. The magical element, it is true, has disappeared in the process of time, but the sacerdotal element has maintained its place both in the theory and practice of the criminal law.

The purpose of medicine is no longer a controversial question. The purpose of medicine is the healing of the sick. But the fact that it is still regarded as heresy to investigate the purpose of criminal law shows how firmly criminal law is anchored in atavistic conceptions; according to which the application of the notion of causality to those who infringe the law is wrong because, unlike his bodily functions, man's actions are not subject to natural law.

126

Just as we regard the healing of the sick as the general aim of medicine, subject to the consideration that even the most drastic mutilations are ' healing ' as long as life itself is preserved, so one could describe the purpose of penal law as being the social adaptation of the individual. This adaptation will take the most different forms, from legal pressure on the imagination of the potential criminal, which we call deterrence, to the extinction of physical existence, as a last resort. With the idea of social adaptation appears, however, a moment of uncertainty. In a time of chaos and social remodelling we have seen the most different types of States and communities arise. It is, however, impossible for criminal law to be based on a principle, which appears to contradict itself and has not the character of permanency.

So we must embark on the search after a principle that is independent of changes of time and place.

The Theory of Selection

The most that one can do is to compare and enumerate the single aims of deterrence, reform, preventive detention and curing, for their reciprocal relationship remains dark and indistinct. But the establishing of this equivalent is just what matters, and this is only possible in a unitary theory.

It is possible, perhaps, to find such a ' roof ' idea in the development of research into the Darwinian hypothesis, which the great scientist advanced over the performance-enhancing function of natural selection.

According to the Darwinian hypothesis, Nature automatically selects all minus variants for destruction, but useful variants of the organism persist and consolidate themselves. Self-injurious variations fall victims to the hostile forces of the world around them and disappear.

127

PUNISHMENT

One could argue, too, the other way round: that which is unable to preserve itself is, as a rule, a minus variant. That which remains alive must be biologically valuable. This, of course, can only refer to unaltered conditions of environment, that is, those not deformed by human interference, but also conditions of the surrounding world which do not exceed the normal capacity for adaptation of living creatures. Catastrophes, such as earthquakes or volcanic eruptions, and the extreme variations in climate that have occurred in the course of geological time, do not call for consideration. In such cases the higher animals (and man) have no procedure of survival but migration to a less hostile area.

It is not unfair to say that the doctrine of natural selection implies an essentially anthropomorphic conception of nature. Darwin without doubt had the idea suggested to him from one of man's most valuable discoveries, the subjection of whole, large groups of animals, which are withdrawn from free life and autonomous existence and placed in the service of man. They no longer live for themselves, but for their breeder. They must nourish him, defend him, watch over him and act as a means of locomotion for him; their servitude makes him more than anything else master of nature.

Animals could only be made domestic gradually, by bringing them, once their rudimentary social instincts had developed, into man's proximity in the most social phase in their lives, viz., youth. Further, in order to dull their pugnacious propensities, it was necessary that the animals should not have to struggle for existence (which struggle is primarily concerned with nourishment and self-defence) or for mates. The animals which man regularly supplied not only with food, but also with sexual partners, lost the warlike attributes on which

128

their life in a free preserve rested. They could in part keep their youthful attachment and in part develop new features of attachment which found their object in man, the substitute for the mother which nourished and protected them.

This rebreeding of mentally unformed animal-breeds depended on systematic selection. Animals in which the old wildness broke out intractably and irradicably must not be allowed to breed, while those animals in which clear tendencies and progress were evident, must be carefully encouraged to breed.

Such was the origin of the domestic animal. Besides the free, independent animal organism equipped with pugnacious attributes, there emerged the controlled animal, dependent on man's feeding and protection, and charged rather than equipped with attributes of utility. There came about a symbiosis in which the animal developed to the limit of its own vitality functions that were useful to man. But the benefit of these functions could only be acquired in return for a counter service; man granted the creature, which had sunk back into childish helplessness, protection against the hostile powers of nature and his free and predatory animal kin. Only in a few cases, where the creature's efficiency consisted of a certain watchful combative action (e.g., the dog) did man try to combine obedience with wildness through a careful process of crossing and recrossing.

The family as a natural defensive unit was the pattern of this symbiotic division of labour between man and beast; but the family is for ever being founded and broken up. The attachment of children is an expression of the purest helplessness, and, apart from any objective usefulness of young children, only felt subjectively in one's deepest emotions, in the instinctive gratification of impulse. The family came into being, grew and disappeared. With the independence of the young animal, with the first unfolding of his strength, and the first welling up of the sense of his power, the bond of affection was dissolved as something unnecessary, useless, and even injurious.

The man-beast symbiosis was, on the other hand, free from this tendency to crumble away. True, many feelings which had lost their object, remained as a kind of incrustation, but the lasting and certain foundation was mutual indispensability. Should this rational relationship be called in question as regards the weaker (*i.e.*, the animal) because of some disparity between the amount of food and efficiency owing to the development of injurious or troublesome attributes (of which old age is always one), then the possessor rids himself of the burden by destroying it and using up the organic animal remains. In the family the youth became stronger and stronger, and was finally hardly conquerable; while the animal breeder could strive towards purer and purer efficiency types with ever renewed acts of selection ruthlessly carried out, because man's superiority was never seriously challenged. He was the stronger, was master of life and death, of food and mate, and thus despotic tyrant of every act of breeding.

The domestic animal, as we know it to-day, has lost that unruly element in its nature which enabled it in the wild state to fight for prey and mate. Only when in heat does the animal still resume for a few days the tradition of freedom which has otherwise been bred out of it. And even this last relic of an independent animal nature is tolerated by the breeder, only because, though troublesome to him, it is symptomatic of fecundity and a profitable new generation of beasts. Besides, this animal

130

slave can live only as long as the protection of his master lasts. Should the close symbiotic association be broken, the man can at a pinch continue to live, but his beast must perish, having been deprived of the qualities that fit him for a competitive existence.

If the breeder by artificial methods of selection has succeeded in turning self-supporting, independent wild animals into members of a great community of creatures who are fit to live together, we easily come to the idea of giving criminal jurisdiction a similar task. With its entire arsenal of light and massive means criminal jurisdiction must work out a type of man who fulfils the conditions of human symbiosis.

There is, in fact, no more certain guarantee of cohesion in a group than harmonious psychical reactions among its members.

The public is apt to regard purposive pairing in breeding with alternating repulsion and enthusiasm. Such a thing, however, is outside the scope of criminal jurisdiction, as, too, is the giving of a positive incentive, or reward, for any desired behaviour. In every sphere of cultural life it is both recognized and customary to attempt to further a desired human type, but the question of reward only occurs in penal law when certain factors allow of mitigation in the execution of a punishment.

Thus criminal law can carry out only a negative selection. It can, like an artificial earthquake, forcibly given sickness, artificial famine and winter, lower the conditions of the existence of an individual. By this shortening of life, which may be the slightest of influences or destructive blows, that type of man is affected whose attributes, like crenated stones shaped without plan, hinder the formation of a compact and cohesive society.

If the untamed, unproductive, the ' wild ' variety of man gradually disappears, with incessant selection, there will come about a race of men having a socially constructive kind of psychical reactivity.

The penal laws of every country and age have certainly worked out a certain type of man by their subjection of everything which seems injurious or troublesome to them; and the society whose instinct showed it clearest what was socially really injurious has the longest maintained itself in the struggle of peoples and races.

By ordering all penal measures under the highest aspect of social selection, the old arrangement of purposes, reform, deterrence, preventive detention and curing will not be superfluous. We will only have to show how these subordinate aims come into line with the idea of selection.

Reform

The peoples early began to provide themselves with guarantees against the threats contained in the everlasting authority of penal law and its administrators. The words ' legal security ' suggest that justice like every other power of heaven is dreadful, " when it disengages itself from the fetter " and, a free daughter of Nature, steps into the track of force. The principle of legal security opposes any rapid and more or less arbitrary decision over the social worthlessness of a person. This principle, however, is also in everlasting conflict with a perfected selective function of the State. One can equally well see in the slight, preliminary methods of selection, which one calls reform, an effect of the desire for legal security.

Here we suddenly find ourselves in the midst of the fundamental problems of punishment. The facts of the case in punishable actions were set down in abstract

132

stiffness, because it was desired to let the arbitrariness of the people who judge only vent punishment on those characteristics of the perpetrator which were marked in certain external happenings and in determinable and demonstrable states of will. The facts of a case of criminal law, when they are realized in life, form the pointer to a certain form of anti-social tendency from which actions of that type generally break out. In this, penal law can only arrive at the average, it must frequently invent that rigid-ideal relation between deed and situation when it is lacking in the individual case, the exceptional case.

Thus the judgment of delicts against property supposes a dishonest and subduable intention of appropriation, which, according to its moral accentuation, rests on the assumption of normal industrial conditions and normal possibilities of work. One always thinks of the contrast of honourable work and dishonourable appropriation, and not of the contrast of threatened self-preservation and theft through necessity. The ethically strongly accentuated assessment of theft springs from the simpler and easier conditions of earlier times. But, if to-day millions are left unemployed and by an accident, such as sickness or previous imprisonment, the modern State's mechanisms of assistance cease to function or are abolished, then the same act of theft has a quite different psychological worth from that of the same deed in normal or favourable industrial conditions.

In these cases it is not the object of selection which has altered, it is the barometric conditions of the world around which have changed. Penal law is here not justified in taking severe measures, because no traces of actually criminal characteristics have appeared, but the instinct of self-preservation has reacted in the external form of what constitutes a criminal act. If criminal law must here, too, decide on certain punitive effects, then it can find a justifying aspect only in the sphere of the deterrent. At any rate it will make use of measures of reform. The most energetic ' reforming ' effect would be to direct its efforts against the criminal-breeding conditions of life which should be washed away like a swamp which breeds germs of infection.

In exactly the same way punishable actions on the part of youths signify something quite different from a symptom of a definitely fixed tendency. These are rather to be regarded as faulty attempts at walking in the experimental phase of life, in which youth plays its way through life with a plastic mind and body fit for exercise, and should learn as it plays.

In every case where there is capacity for reform, radical measures of selection would be an irrational over-haste which would unnecessarily and uncritically deci-mate the available breeding material of the modern civilized State, and would reproach the breeder with bungling. Reform, then, whether by means of simple education, reformative punishment, or improving the *milieu*, aims at preserving material by mild, corrective and bloodless means, like the conservative methods of the medical man. Before the State interferes with destructive selection, it contents itself with experimental measures of selection.

We can reckon as reformatory all interference which, without shock to or twisting of the mental ' movable axle,' influences people who are corporally and intel-lectually completely socially adjustable. The great danger of pure compulsory punishment lies in the fact that it leaves behind cracks, inflammations and weals in the psychic structure, like a medicament which has a toxic action as well as the desired advantageous effect it obtains and therefore in one case improves, but in another organic system has an injurious effect. Reform presupposes a certain plasticity. If the individual is accessible to the corrective interference which alters functions, then the process of selection stops at this step. It has itself shown that the employment of stronger methods cannot be justified in regard to the object as much as in regard to economy of its own strength.

Deterrence

The effects of selection which penal law obtains by intimidation, are not essentially more efficacious. As a psychological attempt to exercise compulsion, intimidation works in two directions. An association between the action threatened with punishment and the painful consequences of the action can only be established in the mind and emotional life of the punished person as a result of simple infliction of pain.

In relation to reform, it is here more the effects of the pure infliction of pain which are brought to the fore, in contrast to measures which form, or grind away, habits and in which, in order not to break the connexion between educator and educated, it is desirable that they should only slightly be consciously concerned with pain.

Man's capability of being deterred is no constant unit, but differs according to age, sex, race, climate and the position of the individual in his sexual periods. Here many external factors show very great effect; thus a man in a crowd, which excites him and numbs him with its weight, becomes momentarily completely fearless. With sufficient motive, fear is a normal, biologically valuable, psychic reaction; in contrast to this we observe a lack of fear or slight remnant of fright, in many lunatics

135

with sluggish nervous systems which are difficult to excite. Everybody knows that the healthy reaction of fear can be practically stifled by certain nervous poisons.

I once said that it would be juster to remove the mental armour and create great sensitivity to pain than continually to increase the calibre of the State's mechanisms of bombardment, as was done with such obvious failure in the sixteenth and seventeenth centuries. For every living being is able to defend itself against the stimulus of pain by steeling its mind, stupefying the pain-conveying channels and nervous centres. It was without doubt the fundamental error of all ages, which through their own timidity fell back on pure intimidation as was done in the time of the later Roman Emperors and the later Middle Ages, that man was regarded as something immutable and unprovided with internal powers of resistance, and in this it was forgotten that man, like every living creature, is able to overcome pain in the receptive organ by means of stronger conceptions or to let himself be choked. In the competition between the infliction of pain and its exclusion by the tormented, penal law was in the end defeated because its punitive methods had become unbearable to it and could not be borne by the State.

Thus pure intimidation as a fundamental principle of punitive politics is doubly injurious. It demands from the State an ever-increasing expenditure of force, which, however, with increasing infliction of pain, is not converted into increasing pain, but in indirect proportion to the brutality of the means used engenders that which one could perhaps call ' swallowing ' pain. As a motive-forming moment it is rendered inefficient.

Compared with reform, intimidation is an irrational principle, because there must gradually arise a large disparity between expenditure of force and effect. This disparity is clearly seen when we consider that side of intimidation which is directed against man's instinctive fright. Every punishment exacted, it is said, strikes the hovering instincts of those who without this warning would have become criminals.

It would pay us to investigate more closely whether this assumption is right. Such weighty questions of social life cannot be resolved with a simple dictum. At the most one can turn one's glance back and ransack the ages in which firmly operative deterring pressure of the law court and punishment was put an end to by conditions in which this social defensive mechanism no longer functioned, or only incompletely so. If one considers the great French Revolution or the year 1848, one sees that the great mass of the population, even without a directly founded fear of law and justice, did not leave the path of legality. There are regularly certain groups of criminals or mentally unbalanced persons who unleash their criminal tendencies under the cover of the preliminary chaos of a revolution or equally of a reactionary movement. It is worth noting in this connexion that these types regularly seek for their actions the actual or ostensible cover of a political object or purpose of social reform. So far as our experience goes, the deterrent effect of punishment cannot be denied all influence in regard to the mass of the population; its effect is, however, far and away not so large as is generally assumed nor as that with which our passionateness, stretched to bursting point and demanding liberating nervous discharge, dazzles our eyes, in order to be able to prepare for the relieving counter attack.

One must not forget that behind the organized, but by no means omniscient or omnipotent, power of punishing of the unshaken structure of the State stands the unregulated, but partly very powerful, defence of the smaller group and of the individual. As soon as the State for a short time resigns its function of defending the law, other improvised protective structures are formed and step into the breach. In any Revolution one sees organizations of self-defence immediately appearing. At first in the country where the property instinct is most strongly developed and the obtusest peasant knows that the eternal war between man and man, which the State has otherwise forced into still and legally embanked channels, has suddenly wakened up in all its wildness and can only be warded off with physical means.

It would be important to find out whether it is just the severity of the threatened punishment which affects human prudence and whether the fact that a deep gulf lies between threat and execution, does not make the severity of the threat illusory for many people who are sure of themselves, their strength and cleverness, or also who are unconscious of their stupidity.

There are still other considerations. The religious person believes firmly in the omnipotence and omniscience of God. God looks into the hidden and sees every crime. Here punishment is closely connected to the deed done. Yet even these people commit crimes. and, indeed, for the sole reason that at the moment of the deed the motive-forming force of religious remonstrance is small. This momentary weakness originates in the fact that, according to the belief of many people, divine punishment does not take immediate effect, but will only be exacted for certain after death. However the suspended evil of punishment has, as it seems, only a slight effect on many people, because from experience of everyday life, the intersecting interference of casual

138

events, which an anthropomorphous conception of God can never quite get rid of, will come in.

This practical washing out of the harshest threat of punishment is joined finally by a moment of criminological nature to which we, in times of highly developed mechanisms for throwing out profitable suggestions like the press and wireless, have only now learned to pay more attention. The emotional culture of a people, its refinement or blunting, will also be affected by the way in which the State exercises its power of punishing. The State which threatens cruel punishments puts cruel ideas in the heads of the people. These ideas have a repulsive as well as an attractive effect. The brutal State makes the majority of people equally brutal, as it tries to intimidate a small, dangerous minority. It is an old experience that beaten children make beating fathers, that a police which shoots, makes criminals ready to shoot, and that in the cruel State, without it wishing or noticing it, there grows up a cruel population, an incessant circle of brutalities which at the end usually turns into injudicious, self-subversive ' humaneness.'

The history of psychiatry teaches us that the idea of deterrence has also dominated the treatment of the sick, originally forcing its way slowly out from the lunatic asylums. This development allows us to foresee that in time penal law, too, will cut out the idea of intimidation as a dangerous and even poisonous ingredient and reduce it to a very modest measure. The tendency to deterrent reactions belongs to the forms of instinctive behaviour which in narrow private life and to a small extent also in public life are able purposefully to regulate social life. but which must be put out of service, when in complicated conditions instinctive treatment by the State does more harm than good.

PUNISHMENT

Kraepelin tells of the curious method of the psychiater Reil who, in connexion with Pinel's ideas, taught that above all one must break the disobedient element latent in the disease, in order to make the patient accessible to medical influence. When one reads these treatises, one is forcibly reminded of methods which many people even to-day defend and use in the execution of punishment. Reil says: " By means of strong and painful impressions we extort the attention of the patient, accustom him to unconditional obedience and indissolubly impress in his heart the feeling of necessity. The will of his master (!) must be for him a law so firm and unalterable that it as little occurs to him to disobey it as to fight against the elements."

Here in the realm of the art of healing appears the need for a severity which, as we know, has in changing degree dominated whole periods in history. However, if Reil's desire is to make the patient so helpless as to give up in discouragement the struggle against the elements, then one may object that the life of every animal and many people consists of an incessant, often victoriously carried out, struggle against the elements which are as little unconquerable as the will of another person.

To-day in the nursing of the insane as much as in the infliction of punishment we attribute substantial importance to the building up of an unbroken self-respect. The systematic shaking of self-assurance belonged to the earlier method of intimidation, for a diseased state of mind was traced back to a consciously hardened evil will, to a morally reprehensible refractoriness. For this reason Reil proposed to bring the patient to an asylum which he did not know, with ceremonious and terrifying scenes, making detours and where possible by night. " As he approaches he hears the beating of drums, the thunder of cannon, he drives over bridges hung in chains, and is received by Moors. An entrance under such ominous forebodings can on the spot destroy any projected refractoriness."

Surprising coercion alternates with sudden friendliness; but above all strong, unexpected impressions must assail the patient and produce in him the feeling of complete helplessness. " For example, the patient is brought into a vault, pitch dark and deathly still; filled with the strangest objects, fixed and moveable, dead and alive; such as, when terrifying impressions are required, bags filled with air, gargoyles, pillars of ice, fur-men, marble statues, dead hands which stroke the beard without being seen. Also there shall be the crackle of squibs, pistol shots, the thunder of cannon, the shrill note of a wind instrument, the continuous roar of a 32-foot organ pipe, single beats on the Turkish drum, a wild mixture of drums, shawms, human voices, howling of animals, a cat piano. Theatrical performances showing executions and the dead returning from the grave, shall work on his sight; here Don Quixote would be knighted, imaginary pregnant women relieved of their burdens, lunatics trepanned, remorseful sinners ceremoniously remitted their crimes."

According to our present-day ideas, such a doctor would have to count himself among his own patients. Here it is, however, the medical thought of his age, the conception of mental disease as a fault of will which can be stripped off, which speaks to us with a certain richness of phantasy. Are we not reminded of certain ' new ' doctrines in penal law?

No scientific psychiatry could develop as long as the disease was something which had no cause, which was produced by evil will and curable by breaking that evil will. When inquiry is made into the causes of crime and these causes are attacked, criminal jurisdiction will, too, rise to the heights of the tremendous successes of modern medicine. To-day it is still an ingeniously built-up logical system of rules which are of magical or superstitious origin and nowhere rest on the firm ground of the recognition of causal reality. It is just this uncertainty which continually leads to the return to mass emotion and its demands; that assures the idea of intimidation its unbroken predominance.

Reform and intimidation are preliminary steps in the social process of selection which lead to massive measures of elimination should it turn out that more superficial interference has not led to social adaptation. Intimidation, however, penetrates, as a subsidiary aim, as far as those methods of punishment with which the State directly attacks life and destroys life or procreative ability. But, first, there intrudes yet another variant of selection, which keeps the mean between conclusive methods of punishment and those which can be compensated or at least gone through by doing time. We regard safe custody as a safeguarding measure along with sterilization and the death penalty.

Preventative Detention

If we discover in reform and intimidation preliminary, hesitant and revisable forms of social selection, then with preventative detention, with life-long imprisonment, drastic corporal interference and the death penalty it is a question of conclusive selective measures. The person who is interned in prison or an asylum until he dies, is, it is true, not immediately eliminated, but he is subjected, as a source of social danger, to treatment which practically is the equivalent of elimination.

In the forefront is complete isolation of the individual from free life. The possibility of conflict with his surroundings is confined to the very smallest possible space. The life prisoner is kept away from any procreative possibility. He is ' killed ' only that this destruction is undertaken with bloodless means not directly nor in active form, and thus has the appearance of being a gift of life.

Several considerations intersect here. From the point of view of humaneness such a decade-long theft of freedom can scarcely be called a method of euthanasia. From the point of view of political economy such treatment is costly and little productive. From the point of view of pure security in one or the other case an attempt to escape may succeed, although practically only those attempts come into consideration which do not end, as does the majority, in early recapture.

In regard to this there is the fact that the possibility of reviewing an unjust sentence remains open, and, further, such a method of treatment takes one of the strongest of cultural theses, the inviolability of human life, into consideration. Without doubt in cases of lifelong preventative detention the legal possession of human freedom, too, is sensibly affected and injured. This lesser evil, however, must be submitted to with the rest, because without deprivation of freedom and without coercion the more valuable public security cannot be maintained. We infringe man's freedom in other cases too, where there are grounds for justification, in the education of children, the cohabitation of man and woman, mental disease, in war and many forms of bodily sickness which are dangerous to the community. In all these cases the departure from the rule of man's ability to move freely is based on the higher purposes of social life.

There exists, to be sure, one danger. However much man's legal consciousness, behind which perceived threat and startled parry hide, bubbles up when excited by a crime, and demands destructive forms of punishment, this sentiment, fed on the emotions of the moment, subsides again as quickly. Impulses of tender-heartedness appear, for simple people—and there are many simple people in every stratum of society—react quickly to the deed, the momentary danger, and are incautious and inactive in regard to remote danger or the danger which lies hidden in the constant peculiarities of an individual. From this there comes the tendency to show mercy after a length of years, without consideration of whether actual reform or harmlessness has been brought about. Here a perfectly straight course must be steered, those who are capable of reforming must be recognized and not condemned to lifelong imprisonment. In the case of the really dangerous criminal, however, commiseration must be ruled out, having absolutely nothing to do with dangerousness. He remains shut up until he has become innocuous. It is often old age or other corporal revolutions which first give this guarantee.

The most energetic form of safeguarding was and is the death penalty. We have followed the punishment up from its earliest beginnings and will later examine details still closer. The death penalty greatly resembles the methods of the animal breeder, who kills undesired specimens. If we consider the figures of the executions in great civilized countries—say, England and France—then we are forced to recognize that the death penalty's brutal selection has lost all practical importance. It is only the psychological part, the threat

144

of punishment, which is still used. At any rate, in considering the effect of the persisting threat, we must not forget that all statistics suffer from great incompleteness. I think that there is no crime less discovered and more seldom punished than murder. The criminal police would have better results, in Germany, France and England, if they would admit this fact without being touchy about it, investigate it minutely and thus make a beginning in ridding the world of it.

Besides this elimination of the individual, to which suicide and certain types of fatal accident also belong, there is the old method of germinal elimination, which has now been taken up again and is the subject of much dispute. Sterilization is also carried out naturally by means of the death penalty and life imprisonment. The difference between indirect sterilization and the new technique lies in the fact that we now attack an inferior germinal course without destroying the organism which carries, protects and feeds the sexual apparatus; thus our procedure goes the opposite way, formerly we affected the germ-plasm by destroying its broad corporal base, to-day we preserve the individual existence of the person, but interfere with the procreative mechanism. That is to say, we ignore the criminal tendency in the individual, which blooms and withers with the somatic base, but lay decisive weight on seeing that this tendency does not multiply and is extinguished with its bearer. In quite a similar way the animal breeder prevents the isolated specimen from procreating, even when he does not immediately kill it, while he drives the animal of high efficiency on to increased propagation and carefully chooses suitable sexual partners for it. Social selection does not attack the individual existence but interrups all the more effectively the cycle of the generations.

PUNISHMENT

Curing

There are other sterilizing interferents, quite different from this, which belong to the curative measures. It is not the germinal cycle which is broken off in the first line. Here there are connexions between sexual apparatus and behaviour of the individual, which turn his personality into a social danger. It is not, in this case, the propagation of inferior germs which stands in the foreground, but the undisciplined raging of the sexual animal which is shut up in the cage of his corporeality. The morbidly excited sensuality drags the entire organism with it without the brain being able to exert a restraining influence. It results in attacks on sexual delicacy, the most vulnerable of all legal benefits, on the corporeal integrity of a child or the life of a woman. Under conditions which have to be more exactly determined, surgical interference can here bring about a diminution in impulse and chain up the unruly sexuality again.

This curative treatment is in character nothing else than the removal of a thyroid gland or malicious tumour. Here sterilization, considered in the light of racial hygiene, is only a secondary result. Of first consideration is the liberation from an organically founded source of biochemical incentives which in the first place attack man's brain and morbidly over-intensify his copulative appetite. Because another person is, as a rule, necessary for copulation, there arises danger for the community.

It is interesting that not always, but in the great majority of cases, the surgeon does not only tie up or extirpate a corporeal organ, but in doing so also revolutionarily interferes with what even to-day our penal law calls ' free will.' Our laws deny this corporeal

146

dependence at the same moment as they recognize this alliance by permitting the operation.

With the advance in our knowledge, curing ' in itself ' means in a great number of cases contra-selection. What is the position with regard to the curative inter- ference of surgical, medicinal, organo-therapeutic and other methods with which we are to-day already able to resocialize, and in future to a very great extent will be able reformatively to reconstruct many people. There is without doubt the same danger as in purely medicinal curing, for we alter the people in their profoundest elements, in what they are and what their children will be, just as little as an ugly woman makes herself beauti- ful with the perfect application of cosmetics. What then is the purpose of taking all these pains?

We will again come up against the same anxious ques- tion in regard to lunatics. At any rate a careful selec- tion is demanded. A biological minus variant can be culturally valuable and thus in a roundabout way be socially good for a conservable amount. Besides, cura- tive measures can take the place of punishments, which would demand much more personal effort and positive expense; so they are sometimes indicated by considera- tions of economy. However, the great principle of helping man by curing him can only be carried out in absolute unconditionality. I think that the harm it does is far less than its power of preserving life and happiness.

3. Faulty Selection

The Gap in the Idea of Guilt

The powerful selective apparatus of penal law is no perfect construction. When responsibility was made dependent on the assumption of a free will, the selective system was broken through. While in every other sphere of life the mode of thinking of causality was applied to phenomena of life, a causative connexion between criminal will and punishable success was indeed admitted; but the threads of causal connexion were cut behind the free will. The will is its own cause, without origin; no causal bond leads from it to the incessant interaction of natural tendency and *milieu*. According to the supposition which to-day still dominates our penal law, the criminal's will is free, even were he born in chains. He is the only phenomenon without a cause which exists in the realm of creation.

To have given this will a faulty turn, by means of a kind of ' over-will,' is guilt. The guilt is attenuated or disappears according as there become visible in the free genese of will individual features which we know as causal from other conditions of life. Such causal connexion between determination and determinants is taken for granted by penal law in cases of mental derangement. In former centuries one called the personification of this cause ' devil.' Therefore as soon as free disposition of will is brought to an end by a clinically more or less known process of disease, there is no place for penal law.

With the idea of irresponsibility it is a question of complete suppression of the freedom of will. Other factors develop weaker effects in the will's genese; such moments can come from natural tendency or emanate from the surrounding world. In the case of such a ' half ' causality one speaks of lessened responsibility, if it appears on the side of the natural tendency and if our medical experience comprises such disorders.

On the other hand, we speak of mitigating circumstances when slight causal connexions, such as hunger

148

or exhaustion, or any serious family conflict, lead from the world outside to the will. To this also belongs provocation by the victim himself in cases of manslaughter or rape.

In all these cases penal law has not found its way out from the conflict between old moralizing conception and increasing recognition of the causal conditionality of every psychic reaction, naturally also of an action of will. The solution which was first developed in the case of the insane, or better, which has been retained from olden times, consists in taking the mentally disordered criminal out from the penal selective process, without substituting it by another method.

Now it is certainly right and acknowledged by the coincidental praxis of every nation, that the mentally disordered shall not be subjected to pure penal punishment, because as a rule punishment has no effect on them.

On the other hand, the dangerousness of such patients persisted beside the disease or just because of it. As the patient was rightly spared the methods of penal punishment, then one must have brought other selective mechanisms into use. These means could be directed against the occurrence of the disease, in so far as a therapy has been found at all up till now. If the disease was curable, then the mentally disordered person ceased to be an object of selective efforts on his being finally cured.

The incurable madman must be subjected to that stronger selective influence which lies in long lasting confinement, that is, preventative detention. Countless difficulties have arisen from the fact that mental disorder is an occurrence which often progresses in leaps and bounds, often seems to stop and then, suddenly relapsing, destroys the entire deceptive picture

149

of improvement. The asylum is conceived as a place of cure and care for the mentally disordered, thus the psychiater is inclined, quite rightly from the point of view of the aim of his calling, to dismiss the patient if his condition improves; for safe custody is not the task of the asylum. It is true that the patient is put back again at the first sign of relapsing, but this sign is very often a crime.

Just like the prison, the asylum implies the minimum of incentive from the surrounding world. In the conflictlessness and calm of the asylum a person will often show no clear signs of sickness, but when he steps out into free life with its countless noxious manifestations, with its ruthless attacks on the body and psyche of the person who has been cured, the sickness immediately becomes active again. The smouldering process of disease breaks into flames on contact with the oxygen of real life.

The insane criminal, because he is diseased, belongs to the asylum. His dangerousness to the community destines him for detention or, as long as we have no such measure, to the convict prison. To-day, under the influence of the idea of guilt, we neglect the preventative protection. We assign the sick person to the hospital which has no right to detain the person who has been cured. Thus there is no question of a rational defence against dangerous personalities; we must either entrust the psychiater with protective functions and duties or we should extend the curative treatment into penal detention. As things are now we have delineated two sharply separated circles of treatment which admit of a ' no man's land ' between them, and it is just in this intermediate sphere, where there is no treatment, that countless delicts are committed.

All these difficulties are, in the case of criminal

lunatics, still surmountable, because, besides the convict prison, which is declared incompetent, there is still the lunatic asylum which absorbs at least a proportion of the lunatics for at least a certain length of time. On the other hand, the contradiction between moralizing interpretation and causal consideration of crime has been raised to its full height in cases of lessened responsibility. Various causal features, woven into the collective picture of free will, are recognized here, but only in such a way that the will still passes for free, though less free. Correspondingly guilt ' abstractly ' suffers an attenuation, without there being anything certain to show the degree of this diminution.

Thus the psychopath, for example, a psycho-pathological type which is particularly frequently found among chronic criminals, is regarded as less guilty of his actions. The practical result of extenuated guilt is a reduction in punishment. That is to say, people who, because of their tendency to relapse into the worst forms of crime, are particularly dangerous and so should be subjected to a particularly severe selection, are submitted to particularly ineffectual and intentionally weakened methods of selection. In judicial praxis one proceeds like a doctor who, as the fever rises, reduces the dose of quinine. The less responsible can propagate without limit and because of the shortness of the punishment they cannot even be educationally sufficiently lastingly influenced; they are not deterred by the reduced punishment and, finally, the short-term punishment cannot be considered as having any protective effect. The devastation which is caused here cannot be done away with by separating the questions of guilt and security, retaining the shortened punishment and at the same time taking police measures in the shape of preventative detention. The problem cannot be solved by a division in which one seeks to save old ideas which have become dangerous to the community by a quite unnecessarily complicated combination of poison and antidote. If it is a fact that the mentally inferior, the psychopath, who is not yet, or no longer, insane, cannot be reformed or deterred by punishment, then he should be detained indefinitely. Should one wish to use short punishment and detention collaterally, then one should arrive at the same result as the English practice. The legally permissible preventative detention would be more and more forgotten. The judge, with complete justice, considers only one method of treatment right. Because he cannot order detention by itself, he gives penal servitude by itself, which he extends a little in order to attain the effect of a longer detention.

We lend our support to the idea that penal law comprises a system of methods of social selection which gets its information from a catalogue of socially especially injurious or troublesome actions, the penal code. Because of the ruling doctrine of guilt and extenuated guilt, a yawning breach has been made in the defensive front of penal jurisdiction through which crime thrusts itself into complete or extensive immunity. If irresponsibility means no punishment and lessened responsibility slighter punishment, then one must recognize that in principle the medical question of psychosis or mental deficiency cannot deprive penal law of the duty of protecting in an extensive manner the community from these two dangerous types. The actually indicated, but unworkable selective method of punishment must be replaced by another modality of selective treatment: for lunatics protective measures, coupled with the attempt to cure them, for the less responsible as a rule detention, at

least efficient superintendence from which educational
or medical efforts to help them should not be excluded.

The entire fiasco of our criminology in relation to real
crime is due to the fact that this breach is closed neither
by a simple leading idea nor by any simplified, effective
measure of State. The further psychiatry advances and
the more it succeeds in regarding man's formation of will
as a causal course and in dividing it up into its causative threads and in inserting into these causal relation-
ships processes of sickness or degeneration which are
exactly known, the more severely is the idea of guilt
shaken, and the greater, with the duration of the mystics
ruling at present, will be the wrong result which appears
accusingly before us in the figures of criminal statistics.

Punishable actions can be forced out of a relatively
social disposition by the pressure of outside circumstances, just as the healthy body can be made sick by
a very evil climate or the attack of virulent bacteria.
In cases of exogenous delicts, we also speak of extenuated
guilt, which, however, we take into account beside the
unshaken freedom of will. To-day we still punish the
minor guilt of the criminal psychopath and the minor
guilt of the person turned criminal through necessity
in exactly the same way, that is to say, with punishment and, it is true, with slighter punishment.

This similarity of treatment is obviously a great mis-
conception. In the case of the less responsible we are
confronted by criminal tendencies which are often not
accessible to punitive treatment and must therefore be
attacked with other protective methods, detention. In
the case of the person turned criminal through suffering
—suffering in the sense of that exterior pressure which
considerably surpasses the average level of the outside
stimuli—the action of will is started from outside. In

criminal jurisdiction we try to influence the mental disposition in which only slight or no defects are visible. Certainly we must demand from everyone a certain power of resistance against pressure and impulse; if this normal resistance is lacking, it will show that the disposition is defective. There can, however, result so unusual and so cogent constellations in life that there can be no question of faulty disposition, not even when the issue corresponds to the actual fact of a crime. To use a metaphor: many metals have a high melting point, many a low one. We call those metals with a high melting point hard. If by means of a very high temperature we melt a hard metal, we cannot suddenly classify it as soft because it has succumbed to an exceptional temperature. It is similarly so with man's natural disposition. If under very severe pressure from outside circumstances a man has made himself liable to punishment, then the general and often just conclusion: " Crime = Symptom of a defect in social disposition " goes wrong, and the selective proceeding which is built up on this unjust equation goes equally wrong.

If then one can see the beginning of a purified way of thinking and an improved selection, also in mitigating circumstances, in paroling, in the qualified sentence, then the question of delicts produced by the *milieu* will remain a problem which cannot be separated from the imperfection of every human contrivance, but will allow of its being at least theoretically set in motion, with deeper understanding.

4. PERTURBATIONS IN THE SELECTIVE PROCESS

The conception of penal law as an artificially set-up mechanism of social selection is based on a hypothesis of natural science. In the freedom of nature unfavourable tendencies are culled out by those deadly forces with which every living creature has to fight. Useful tendencies are victorious in this struggle, they remain over, persist, increase and then in their turn enter upon a deadly competition which increases their efficiency. This selective process takes place incessantly. It knows neither interruption nor escape.

In breeding the domestic animal, man puts himself in the place of nature. He sorts out those animals which exhibit harmful characteristics and keeps the variants which are of use to him. The result is a deformity, for corporeal and mental qualities are twisted in a direction which gives the breeder and owner of the animals certain advantageous results, without any consideration as to whether these reactivities are harmful or useful to the animal itself.

In breeding animals, mistakes are possible. They are frequently caused by an excessive greediness on the part of the breeder, who attempts to exploit production at the cost of the living substance, its health and reproductive capacity. But as the question of immediate utility is marked in distinct functions of life, such as milk production, formation of flesh, catching mice, growing wool, watchfulness, &c., and as inferior performance is seldom controversial, the breeder does not make any directly serious mistakes. The mistakes revenge themselves on him too quickly and a new road is quickly taken by acquiring better and unspoiled breeding animals. In the peasant mind even superstitious ideas do not hold out long in the struggle with immediate gain. It is quite different in social selection. This proceeding depends on two fluctuating factors; in the first place, from the fact that a person's anti-social tendency, his dangerousness and unproductiveness have

155

been realized and recognized in a criminal action. The murderer who buries, burns or immures his victim and on whom no suspicion falls, considered in the light of penal law is not a murderer nor an object of selection.

Secondly, the judging of a punishable action and the passing of a sentence depend on the decision of men. For reasons of legal security the verdict of guilty, that is the establishing of social worthlessness, is tied to certain rules. These rules are to protect the defendant from arbitrariness and superior force and exercise the function laid upon them in relation to the guiltless, but also in relation to the guilty, especially in criminal procedure, the onus of proof lies on the prosecutor. There is no doubt but that a large number of intelligent and strong-willed criminals, and also those favoured by luck, succeed in breaking through the selective mechanism of the State at weak spots. In the Middle Ages guilt or innocence, which was decided by divine trial or single combat, lay in physical strength or capacity for mobilizing one's last nervous reserves. These quite simple conditions no longer prevail for our age. But there is still a kind of duel between the perpetrator and the public prosecutor which decides the guilt, and which is fought out in straining every muscle and brain. The type of person who has anti-social tendencies, but who at the same time is biologically of high quality, is still frequently able to break through the enclosure by means of the rules of procedure and its very human administrators.

This fact, which we like to cover up, like the statue at Sais, also accounts for the fact that, taking it all in all, we find in the convict prisons a fairly homogeneous material. We cannot rightly label the people who are here driven together as ' the criminals.' In prison is

156

collected, with a few easily recognizable exceptions, the remains of the selective process of penal law. Without doubt this final product is the lowest stratum in crime, and it would be presumptuous to reconstruct ' the ' criminal from this picture; the punished differ as much from the criminals as the menagerie lion does from the king of the desert, only that the cloak of invisibility hides the undiscovered higher type of offender from us, while we do sometimes come face to face with a real lion. The mesh of penal law's net is not so fine that we could call the selection other than very rough and inaccurate; we must always keep this fact before us, especially when revolutionary times of sudden political movements are continually creating new conditions in authority, on which a certain type of criminal, difficult to discover and to convict, incrusts; the United States are already so conscious of this critical state, that these associations and the question breaking them down are considered a fundamental problem in the struggle against crime.

One forgets all too easily that there is only one front in the battle against crime. It is formed of instances, which live and work each for itself, by the police, the court of law and the prison. We overlook, especially as jurists, that all human material, which is brought before the judge for sentence, can only be brought there by the work of the police. Guarantees for the protection of the individual against the superior strength of the State have been created in criminal jurisdiction and procedure. The chief guarantee for the protection of the community from the criminal lies prior to the judge's activity, in the efforts of the police. The criminal psychologist can go as far as to assert that we would obtain better results with a maximum punishment of ten years' imprisonment, if an ideal police should succeed in clearing up every

157

crime and provide sufficient proof of every punishable action, than with an aggravated death penalty or other severe or very severe means of punishment. But the weakest point in an effective system of social selection lies in the daily battle which the criminal of high biological quality successfully wages against the authority of the State, its laws and officials. No reform of penal law or prison system will obtain—practically—the results at which an authority for the prosecution of crime which was really scientifically organized and led, would arrive.

The fact that penal law has to exercise a dual function constitutes another factor of disorder in social selection. In addition to its actual and essential task of working out a social type of man and suppressing variants which are inimical to society, penal law is used as a means of self-protection by the State or religious rulers' instinct of upholding their position. Every political group in power puts forward its claim to be the only beatific system of government and to have to maintain its position in the interests of the community, that is from an eminently social consideration. From this actual or pretended belief in their social mission every ruling stratum takes its justification for regarding attacks against its predominance an anti-social, wrong action, inimical to the State and for attacking this ' crime ' with the means of criminal punishment.

It is a question here of all sorts of front-rank ideas which have manifestly nothing to do with actual social selection. The struggle between actual and future rulers is in the end decided by the fact of whether a form of government or a political method has been able sufficiently to satisfy the vital interests of a State's community, let us say, protection from outside, equalization of inner tension, sufficiency of food and a share in the blessings of civilization among which, for modern man, one must include a slightly saturated consciousness of one's worth. If a ruling group cannot come up to these demands, then the political attack on its position may spring from a lively social consciousness, and it will always attempt to parry the attacker with the weapon of criminal punishment. It will try to brand him as a social enemy, to make his conditions of life more ruthlessly difficult than those of the real criminal. For the action of the criminal injures an uncertain plurality of foreign interests, but the political opponent shakes the ruler and law-giver's greatest good, power, which is at one and the same time his grazing-ground and his fortress.

Thus more recent efforts have tried to bring the political offender within the periphery of the penal process of selection; even to take a certain psychic state into general consideration with the facts of each case. Radbruch has coined the expression ' criminal-through-conviction ' and demands for him a mild sentence and a milder form of treatment. The common criminal, he has said, stands in contradiction to himself, the punishing State comes to him as the representative of his own better and wiser self. The criminal-through-conviction, however, is not of himself refutable; he stands in opposition to another firm conviction incorporated in the power of the State, which may fight him as its opponent, with every severity, but cannot wish to reform him like a morally unprincipled person.

There is theoretical truth in Radbruch's idea, but it comes into conflict with the realities of human nature, for mild treatment of the offender from conviction could, if one looks further into it, provide a disturbing element in the midst of the improvement in selection which is striven after. Apart from the fearlessness of pathologically excited natures, the threat of severe punishment for political delicts constitutes a valuable selection of people who rise against the ruling group. It is just by raising a grave danger, which only allows of certain psychological types joining the open political fight, that the struggle which would otherwise fluctuate incessantly and cause continual unrest, is confined to certain epochs and to forms of government of a certain inner fragility. A State with a securely anchored structure could recognize the criminal-through-conviction as a legal conception. In revolutionary times he will always remain in the sphere of theoretical discussion. One may, indeed, safely foresee that with the first crack in the foundations of a ruling position which has just been taken by storm, not only will the weapons of penal law be directed with all their weight against the assailant, but also the attempt will be made to give a different moral colour to the motives of the criminal-through-conviction and thus put him on a par with the real criminal. Every such identification with however disgraceful means it may have been carried out, appeals to the blind defensive instinct of the community and releases the quaking ruler from the isolation of pure self-defence. With the destruction of his personal opponent, the ruler no longer protects private or personal interests, but the welfare of the community.

Thus, in spite of all the morality of his motives, State praxis will see in the criminal-through-conviction a person dangerous to it, and will strike with the ruthlessness of a fear which is the more justified the stronger the moral conviction of the internal enemy is. Thus this failure of selection will remain. Often it is just the most social natures, as history shows, the stormbirds of great, approaching developments, who fall victim to the State's selective apparatus, in spite of the fact that this mechanism is actually meant only for the enemies of society. If one does not shun paradoxical considerations, one could say that the certain victory of many such criminals-through-conviction who to-day pass in our imagination as philosophers, founders of religions and national saints, is founded in their destruction. This disordering of selection has changed into a selective effect which will last through centuries.

Selective perturbation occurs finally in judicial error. Like the erroneous diagnosis of an incompetent doctor, the sentence of punishment inflicts a wound on the person which is not indicated by any anti-social characteristic. This derangement is only irreparable in the case of a death sentence, castration and of people who die in prison.

The religious root of punishment disappears from the consciousness of civilized man, although there still remain many traces of it. The doctrine of the moral or lawful principle of retaliation, in which the necessities of our excited feelings were poured into the cooling channel of an ethical principle, was a step forward, but the defective results of this idea have shown that it must be replaced by another guiding idea.

Then came the time when intimidation was put to the fore, because fear was in man's heart and fear always thinks it can protect itself by inspiring fear. Then through the dark clouds of these ideas broke the light of the idea of reform. From individual people it spread to society, its nuisances and many sins and negligences. On all this beautiful Utopian optimism there fell a frost, when Lombroso discovered his born-criminals in the Italian lunatic asylums and spread this genial idea wider and wider until it embraced the entire phenomena of crime. Although his hypothesis may be of the greatest suggestive importance for the understanding of the real criminal, the doctrine of corporeal predestination to crime does not apply to the hundreds of thousands who are forced into punishable actions by the pressure of the world surrounding them, without being more unsocial than the majority of the population which is either not found out in its petty crimes or is not subjected to the same unfavourable influences of *milieu*.

There is perhaps nothing which gives us a deeper insight into the criminal tendencies of a period than that age's system of criminal jurisdiction. As regards the animal, whose efficiency we wish to make use of, we have found a practically objective standpoint of selection. It was preceded by a careful study of the useful animal bodily functions and characteristics and by the investigation of the possibilities which lie, either deleting or strengthening attributes, in sexual union. If here a more certain standpoint was won, then, too, a clear goal was pointed out for the procedure of selection which had to be introduced. I do not know whether the conception of penal law as an organized means of social selection will have a longer life than the old theories; even the discussion of the savants will not come to a decision on this point. In the last instance, practical result, the great arbitrator of every new idea, will decide the issue.

CHAPTER IV

MEANS OF PUNISHMENT

1. Capital Punishment

In the history of their development human contrivances of punishment, like man's brain, eye and heart, rise from lower to higher forms. Their refinement is interrupted by periods of functional simplification; their progress can only be built up on the material at hand, which is being painfully transformed and bears the trace of every error and deformity of the past.

It is from this point of view alone that we must consider capital punishment.

With capital punishment the danger of error is particularly great for two reasons. For some people there is behind the death penalty complete destruction, a nothingness; but for the majority there is the possibility or the certainty of a second life after death, and so it may not be out of the question to make up for a blunder on this earth with reward in the next world or to transform completely the final significance of earthly annihilation by the establishment of a new life.

. Secondly, capital punishment is the oldest means of punishment on earth. The history of its development goes back to primitive times, and we must expect that in our ideas about capital punishment there should still be relics of former stages which are now scarcely comprehensible and have lost all reason or purpose.

If we are to speak about capital punishment, we must be ready to reach back at any time into the palæontology

163

of penal law, which this book has attempted to outline. Behind arguments which lack the foundation of facts, and which go back to necessities of sentiment or metaphysical demands, there is the past which filled the world with magic and charms and invented gods and the sacrificial propitiation of their all too human enmity. Into this atmosphere of the irrational are introduced pseudo-purposes which are nothing but the clumsily or cleverly formulated claims of the emotions or the rudiments of an animistic picture of the world.

The sacrifice of a person whose deed, because of the anger of higher powers, indirectly signifies danger to the community is, to the believer, a highly practical action. The State which shares this belief would neglect its duty of protecting society were it to do away with capital punishment, the only sure means of self-preservation. As long as Christianity was fighting for its existence and stood in blunt opposition to paganism and its use of sacrifices, it repudiated capital punishment, and there was no change in its attitude till after its victory. Luther's depressive character made him as ready for violent reactions as did the social storm of the great Peasant War. Thus he was the most vehement champion of cruel capital punishments.

Thus capital punishment's stronghold in our life is its mystic necessity, an inheritance of long past centuries, whose traces have not yet been completely removed from our brain. Physically we live a double life, civilized in scientific and technical matters, wild and primitive in the things of the soul, which carry the weight of endless periods and changes. That we are no longer conscious of being primitive, makes our tamed kind of wildness all the more dangerous. In the denunciation of capital punishment by the first fathers of the Church there still rings the abhorrence of sacrifice; for God has reserved to Himself the right to dispose of human life and has not given it into the hand of earthly beings. *Ecclesia non sitit sanguinem.* As the Church rose to power and authority, capital punishment was supplementarily intro- duced into the *lex humana* from the revealed law, that is the ancient Mosaic penal law which belongs to another stratum of development. Reprisal and expiation were ideas which replaced the simple connexion between assuasive person and angry deity, but which demanded the death penalty with equal inexorability for every delict deserving of death. But the decision as to whether death was merited came from the same labyrinth of the breast as the belief in magic and anthropomorphous higher powers, which Christianity had replaced by a purified religion. In the collective psychic sickening of witch-madness the judge transferred the ghostly figures of his fearful phantasy to the masses, even to the victim itself, and received, magnified, and coarsened, stirring impulses from the person who had been judged. With the idea of expiation the words were changed, but the social function of capital punishment was in no wise clarified.

So we must remove every metaphysical ingredient from the problem of capital punishment, indifferent as to the form, idea or designation under which they appear. In the most sober computation of all the available, positive elements, we have to answer the question, whether capital punishment is an *effective* means of punishment. We must confront the arguments which speak for this kind of punishment with those which bear witness of injuries to social interests. In capital punish- ment people condemn people to a certain form of treat- ment, which treatment, killing, has not only a physical effect on the condemned, but also a psychical one on the imagination of millions of people. All the effects are accessible to after examination. If they have not yet been made completely clear, then scientific investigation can fill up the lacking experience.

The mistake is made of considering capital punishment ' in itself '; but one can as little divorce a means of punishment from the human category against which it is directed, as one can work with a specific serum against an uncertain plurality of infectious processes. The picture of a disease, which embraces a certain circle of people, is however taken in penal law from the single symptom of a certain wrong action. The crime which in the question of capital punishment alone comes into consideration, is murder.

Two large groups of murderers are automatically to be set aside; insane murderers who, according to the present conception of guilt, may not be killed, and the murderers who, to save themselves from being taken and condemned, commit suicide immediately after the deed. Both categories include the most dangerous types of murderer. Either brutal means are used in killing or there is a plurality of victims.

There is no need to go into the fact that execution would provide absolute security from the remaining grouplets, but what may give rise to doubts is the fact that hundreds of insane murderers are kept secured in another manner, that is in the solid houses of the lunatic asylums.

From the point of view of economy, execution seems to be an ideal method; but one must not forget that the murderer often has a place in the economic process, children, relations, a wife to support. In most cases these people will on the death of their supporter become a burden on public assistance, while the living murderer does not lose his power of working and can take a share in supporting his family.

With these reservations the economy and thorough protective effect of capital punishment can be affirmed; at this point in our investigation the extreme means of punishment shows a plus. The question of reform by means of capital punishment can only arise when one imagines an extension of life after earthly death. Here one looks for a conversion, an act of condensed educa tion, from the shock effect of the last moment. The purified and reformed person continues to live in the next world.

But as penal law does not belong to the realm of faith, but has to do with people and is administered by people, we must leave these uncertainties out of con sideration. Like in medicine or any other method of treating people, we will have to ask whether in capital punishment we must turn to the most primitive and coarsest prescription, the protective, because finer methods, according to the extent of our experience, do not promise resocialization.

Whether murderers are capable of being reformed depends on the causes of the murder and the psychology of the murderer. All those who know the real criminal emphasize the fact that the murderer constitutes a fairly polymorphous group. In murder there come to the fore personal states of conflict, above all those conflicts which are grouped round the sexual sphere. Eighty-one per cent. of all the women murdered in England between 1896 and 1905 were wives or sweet-hearts (239 of the 298 feminine victims of murder). These conflicts have a quite isolated station inside the social structure, from their great majority they are

singular and solitary constellations. Related to the
murderer who tries to solve some conflict with the rough
and unsuitable means of force, there are other types
whose deed is not directed against any certain individual
and always against him alone, but against the interests
of society, these are robbery with murder, rape with
murder, and some other variations. Here one can rather
speak of a general dangerousness which is lacking in the
conflict-murderer; but even here, and especially in cases
of youthful murderers, actual capability of reform, by
means of introducing corporeal and mental maturative
processes, is not out of the question. Between modalities
of crime and capability of reform there is no exactly
determined relationship.

Unconditional safety and cheapness speak for capital
punishment. However, as a considerable number of
murderers are capable of being reformed, and with the
increase of our criminal-psychological knowledge and
insight, murderers will be more justly judged and
treated, and further as we to-day already have in the
solid houses of the lunatic asylums the technical possibilities of forming a detention which is really sure, and
use them, and as the living murderer remains productive
and can be made much more productive still, it would be
a doctor's mistake to take surgical steps where conservative methods can lead to the same result. So there
remains the strongest argument in favour of capital
punishment, its deterrent effect.

Belief in the deterrent power of capital punishment has
two roots; in the first place, there is man's natural
instinct of self-preservation, which is sharper and more
unscrupulous in its reaction, the weaker and more timid
he is. The more such a man is afraid, the more inclined
he is to believe other people to be fearful and the sooner

will he insist on the employment of a means which strikes
to the very root of his soul. There is a miscalculation in
this parallel. The adherents of intimidation, the constitutionally timid, women, the ageing or the ageing social
stratum, fear death and would like the murderer to fear
it too. This is however by no means always the case.
The large number of suicides among murderers points in
a different direction. Very many murderers are only
able to commit the crime because human life, their own
as well as that of others, seems worthless to them. It is
a useless enterprise to try to inflict pain on people so
insensitive to it. In the beginning of December, 1929,
a prisoner who had been condemned to fifteen years'
penal servitude guillotined himself in Sonnenburg
Prison by setting the electric paper-cutting machine in
motion and sticking his head between the knives. In
April, 1929, Faltermeier, who had committed robbery
with murder and was imprisoned at Koburg, hanged himself shortly after having been sentenced to penal servitude
for life. It also says nothing for deterrence when an
executioner is executed or when thieves who have been
hung up as a warning example are robbed by night or the
spectators are plundered by ' deterred ' pickpockets.

For everybody who does not act under the narcotic of
a strong emotion (we expect that in war patriotism without anything further will numb the natural fear of death)
when an evil is threatened, the certainty of its occurring
comes into consideration; it is not the murder which is
punished with death, but the discovered, convicted, and
legally condemned murderer. As only a small percentage
of the murders actually committed are punished, a
strong deterrent effect cannot make itself felt just because
of this barrier.

Added to this is the fact that in those countries which

have legally abolished capital punishment and which
have enjoyed a constant political and social development
(no long severe economic crisis, no revolution, no long,
wasting and brutalizing war), the abolishment of capital
punishment has not been felt as would the removal of a
constant and effective deterrent. On the contrary, the
abolishment of capital punishment has worked like the
removal of a source of crimogenous incentive. In this
we stumble across the kernel of the whole problem of
capital punishment.

Uniformity of thought and action which thrusts
incessant repetition and example on one, is infinitely
stronger than physical coercion. Our age has created
tremendous apparatus for sending out suggestions, in
printing, wireless, and the cinema. He who can penetrate into a person's imagination, who is in a position
to fill it with idols and ideas brought in from outside, dominates that person. He gives no impulse to
the will, but, like a thief in the night, insinuates himself into the subsoil where the will is formed, where conscious comprehension is less sharp. He creeps round
suspicion and prudence, the watchman who instinctively
guards our decisions. In the guise of our own will the
enemy is suddenly within our innermost camp. We have
dragged within our walls another's will, thinking it
booty, like the Trojans and the wooden horse.

All human progress, like every aberration, depends on
such strong suggestions which incessantly bombard our
brain. The possibility of such a seizure of the intellect
has been extraordinarily increased by technical progress.
The wars and revolutions of the last age have been
decided by this, the most imperceptible and dangerous of
all tyrants.

Non-public execution has in this way attained a

publicity of which we can scarcely have an idea. The State's act of killing is impressed on the brains of millions with all the weight of the unusual and the exciting. If there were a sure deterrent effect on the murderous instincts lurking in the dark, then it must have made its appearance. But if there is still another, highly problematical, effect of the State's quiet destruction of life, ceremoniously undertaken, then it, too, must have become evident. I mean an effect of the death penalty, which has nothing to do with the murderer himself, but indeed with the highest duties of the State and the finest criminological means which it has at its disposal.

If claims, such as the inviolability of life, which are fundamentally opposed to the genesis of all healthy life in struggle and defeat, are to win cogent power in people's heads, then they must come in with the magic mien of the absolutely binding. The absolute appeals to the deepest instincts of obedience and the readiness to give way to the higher and stronger, also to the uncomprehended, or just to the uncomprehended, which is implanted in us and drilled into us throughout the centuries. The exception is weakness of the moral position, doubt of the magic force, the badge of an earthly origin, from which all magic powers flee.

Thus the State can only put real life into the principle of the inviolability of life, which it continually and rightly advocates in its reasons for condemning murderers, and in its laws, if it sticks to its own principle, through thick and thin. The State is paramount. If it, the unbridled despot, bows down to the holiness of life, then it has found and brought into use the strongest of all suggestions. To demand this from all will make all the deeper impression, the more the soul of the people in its up and down, from fearful excitement to kind-hearted negligence, suddenly demands a victim, and the more decisively the State, with reference to the inviolability of life, even of the most wretched life, refuses this demand.

People will still go on committing murders. But only the State which, consciously and with all due deliberation, puts up capital punishment like a sword into its sheath, has done everything which lies in its power to protect the citizens from murderous attack by another. It has sent out the most cogent suggestion there is, an example and model of behaviour according to a rule, which may be all the more unconditionally demanded of others, the more ruthlessly one demands it of oneself.

Thus I see in capital punishment a means of punishment whose advantages can be obtained by other means and whose disadvantages can be prevented in no other way than by abolishing it. It is a socially insufficient means of punishment, to which must be added the possibility of a judicial error, which one cannot exclude. This consideration alone would give the criminal-psychologist misgivings about capital punishment, which are not to be allayed other than by dispensing with so risky a practice.

2. CORPORAL PUNISHMENT

Corporal punishment is a moribund means of punishment. Of the civilized European States England is the only one to resist the influences of psychological consideration and practical experience which seek to remove it. In England corporal punishment is admissible for boys under fourteen for all indictable offences, in as far as they come before the Court of Summary Jurisdiction. Judge Hall has established the fact that of the criminal children convicted in the years 1915 and 1916,

35 per cent. had previously been corporally punished, and that this result was more unfavourable than with any other method of punishment. Hall concludes from his, it is true, slight material that corporal punishment must be regarded as the means of punishment which has the least reformative effect and also which deters the least.

Another country, Denmark, has carried out a criminological experiment which is of interest to the civilized world. The Danish judge of the Copenhagen Criminal Court, E. Tybjerg, has given a clear description of the individual stages of this movement. In Denmark several murderous attacks on young girls and the Press's vividly painted, alarming descriptions of them had inflamed the public. The goaded desire of retaliation in which fear and indignation were joined saw in the placid forms of sentencing and the customary methods of punishment a cowardly and lazy reaction which did not release the impulses of rage. "Forbearance and sentimentalism were no longer applied. These beatings had, as it were, something manly and strong in them, and the monsters had richly deserved a thrashing."

After all sorts of struggles the Danish provisional law of 1st April, 1905, was incorporated in the penal code with one or two alterations. Corporal punishment was prescribed as an additional punishment for certain qualified attacks, and for single indecent assaults on young girls. The obligatory character of the subsidiary punishment was lessened by the fact that the judge's free opinion decided on the aggravating circumstances. The proof that the Danish judges and, above all, the highest Danish Court were deeply averse to corporal punishment is furnished by the fact that in the four years (September, 1905, to September, 1909) for which there are statistics, in all Denmark corporal punishment was only inflicted in fourteen cases. On 1st April, 1911, corporal punishment for adults again disappeared from the Danish penal code and took with it corporal punishment as a legal measure against youthful criminals. It is indeed hardly an accident that the original promoter of this brutal and disgraceful punishment, Minister of Justice Alberti, had meanwhile disappeared into prison for fraud and falsification of documents.

In England a similar artificial panic did not meet with the same sudden, instinctive conversion, when in the Criminal Law Amendment Act of 1912 corporal punishment was introduced for souteneurs. I have described a similar attempt which followed on the damaging of the Hohenzollern Memorials in the Siegesallee. As in all similar outbursts of feeling which presume to wish to become law, this petition works with exaggerations of deed and language.

What appeared in the short-lived Danish law and the German petition, which has been followed by others up to the present day, was not an experiment with a new and unknown means of punishment, but the resurrection of a method which since olden days has been used collaterally with capital punishment and other mutilating corporal punishments and which has proved a complete fiasco in the praxis of centuries. Even twenty years ago Thyren pointed out that the proposal to requite brutal crimes with brutal means of punishment such as corporal punishment was psychologically unsound. He rightly emphasized that the more brutal a character is the greater is the likelihood—exceptions granted—of it not being deterred by corporal punishment.

I myself have shown that the cruelty of the crime, which arouses so violent a reaction in our consciousness, is a very complicated idea. As we know, attacks of incomprehensible brutality occur in the initial stages of advancing mental regression. Brutality comes to light after accidents. The brutality shows dependence on age, race, climate and season, fatigue, hunger and the taking of intoxicants. None would wish to say that there is a tendency to brutality inherent in Roman Catholicism, and yet German statistics of crime show that rude delicts preponderate on the Roman Catholic side. The reason might be a combination of the influences of climate, race, economic situation and festive celebration of festivals.

Brutality in attack arouses severity in counter-attack, which severity has two very different objects; neutralization of the opponent and the relief of emotional tension. The supporters of corporal punishment do not take into account that in the modern State there is a substantial interval of time between the deed and the infliction of corporal punishment, in which criminal procedure takes its course. Thus rapid emotional discharge can never be attained, and when sentence has been passed and the corporal punishment is now to be inflicted, feelings are no longer aggressive but have begun to be pacified and are very easily turned into sympathy.

Thus in the problem of corporal punishment there are still two quite reasonable questions. One is: Has corporal punishment a deterrent effect—or to put it better—a greater deterrent effect than other available means of punishment? The second can be formulated as follows: What are the effects of so brutal a means of punishment on the population subject to the laws? Is it protected in its exterior stability, or is it damaged and shaken in its inner moral structure, which is a principal stipulation of exterior stability?

One could make a superficial decision and say that

the course of its development shows that corporal punishment was not really deterrent, otherwise it, which is reasonable, applicable without much apparatus and so to speak omnipresent, would not have disappeared from the penal praxis of civilized peoples leaving only a slight trace. One will not dare to contest the fact that corporal punishment, which for known physiological reasons is regularly more painful for youths than grown-ups, appears externally to make a deep impression. In many cases violent fear of pain is apparent both before and after its infliction. In the case of imprisonment the mental torture of the punishment is spread over a lengthy period and hidden from man's eyes. But without doubt a succession of moments counteracts a lasting impression. Sensitivity to pain is differently developed in different people, in very many cases it is extraordinarily reduced. Sensitivity to bodily pain can be dissipated by repeated or excessive provocation; it is well known that a kind of narcotic is produced by ideas of great strength, which completely displaces the pain from the consciousness and extinguishes it. Finally, bodily pain can even be associated with the sexual sphere and thus receive sexual accentuation which transforms its negative value into an unwished-for positive. Add to this that short but intense bodily pain has, it is true, a strong momentary effect, but does not seem to be particularly suited for building up restraining ideas.

The animal trainer's experience teaches us that the repetition of consciously inflicted bodily pain hinders the formation of ties between trainer and trained, develops a spirit of repulsion, and thus compromises the training relationship. The relation of personal hate which results smothers the objective deterrent effect which is aimed at.

MEANS OF PUNISHMENT

Still more serious is injury to that traditional right of the community which has received recognition and protection, for example, in the cruelty-to-animals paragraphs. The intactness of those feelings on which all civilization rests is nearly as important for the stability of society as public order and safety. The State is not outside the scope of these demands; it is the first to have to satisfy them. For each exception destroys the fetish of inviolable uniformity, which protectively encompasses human life, sexual self-government and also bodily integrity. If it be here objected that freedom of locomotion, movement or unassailability of property belong to the same sphere of legal right, but nevertheless are injured by the State by means of prison and fines, then one may be allowed to say that the State violates and must violate these rights for the sake of a variety of aims: property by raising taxes, personal freedom in the education of children, in the common life of the lawfully married, in the training of soldiers, in the care and sequestration of dangerously or infectiously diseased persons. The infliction of pain which accompanies means of healing has disappeared with the discovery and general introduction of anodyne mediums, and our sensitivity to conscious painful interference in the sphere of the body has been all the more increased.

Thus in corporal punishment I see a crimogenous and thus injurious means of punishment. There is no certain and lasting deterrent of the perpetrator. The only thing certain is the brutalization of the punished, the inflicters of the punishment, the public officials present in their official capacity and especially of the population. I am certain that in a country which generally introduced corporal punishment the number of brutal, criminal actions would increase. The State which sowed a wind, in the shape of this unsuitable means of punishment, would reap a storm.

It is an error to think that measures of state exist insularly for themselves alone. They have exactly the same effect on people's imagination as naughty books and filthy films, whose influence the State itself recognizes and fights against. There is no corporal punishment in our laws, but when the police rubber truncheon, which was originally conceived to replace the naked weapon, was introduced in Germany, beating has forced its way into State praxis with a dangerous weapon. The experience of fourteen years has taught us that when the police are quick to strike, the population too is quick to strike. In the same way the facilitated use of firearms by the police has a criminologically undesired result. The armed burglar has the greatest chance, if he wishes, always to be able to shoot first, and though in Germany very many criminals shoot, the laws on the possession and procuring of firearms have not helped in the least, because it is only the order-loving population which has been disarmed.

I regard the English method of not equipping the police with firearms and thus not only generally suppressing, but also making infamous, any use of pistols or revolvers really clever. Every attack on the unarmed officials is most severely condemned and most draconically punished. To be sure the time has not yet come for the refined criminological conception that an unarmed State is a greater protection than ' energetic ' employment of rubber truncheons which hang at the policeman's side in full view of everybody and revolvers whose leather holsters invite the glances of all. Only when actual experience has shown that these rough, heroic methods are not only ineffective but eventually productive of danger, will a conversion come about of itself. Alone, its perception by a few brilliant brains would never have brought about the change in the methods of penal law, which first stole upon the masses like a dull presentiment of unsuitable absurdities and then found form and expression in the writings of the age of enlightenment. The actual shaking off of an erroneous idea only comes from excessive abuse, as does improvement in the mode of life which we call progress. If we had less fear and ignorance whose most primitive expression is the up-springing of the need for punishment, then we would have pushed back net punishment in a scientific system of treating people into as small a space as surgical interference in medicine.

3. STERILIZATION AND CASTRATION

It is exceptionally difficult to uncouple the punishment from the criminal action and to conform it to the personality of the law-breaker—a task for which our present-day knowledge and methods of investigation are in no way competent; but it is a hundred times more difficult to recognize and judge the germ-plasm and base humane measures on the result of this.

We will not spend much time on the exploration of heredity; heredity is certainly and incontrovertibly an important condition in the building up of mental reactivities. Admittedly the bodily substrata of attributes are invisible, the psychical qualities themselves, as very delicate adaptations to changing outside stimulus, are not, to be sure, to be appraised without more ado as ' good ' or ' bad,' strong or weak, healthy or unhealthy, like muscular strength, eyesight, fertility, &c. Orestes's complaint, that one cannot know by the lance whose soul is heroic, is only one of the examples

179

of this uncertainty. It explains why we judge bodily things comparatively quickly and justly, but always can only define traits of character more closely when a large number of experimental situations have sounded and revealed their psychic reactivity. Unquestionably psychic reactivities are inherited, as has long been shown by animal-breeding praxis and corroborated in the exploration of heredity which is in its beginnings; amongst these must be reckoned a long series of defects or illnesses. By that we do not say that every single trait of the germ-plasm must appear. Their absence can be caused by a peculiarity of structure, their deficiency, however, can be explained by the fact that certain outside stimuli, being absent, have not taxed and activated this trait of character, thus making it visible.

It is disputed whether psychic qualities and defects are inherited according to the Mendelian theory. The risk of inheritance which has been computed in various cases of psychosis, does not yet seem to be scientifically assured. If, on the other hand, both parents show the same type of inheritance, be it characteristic, psychosis or even only strong and similarly directed anti-social tendencies, then we may expect with considerable probability the same trait of character, psychosis or anti-social tendencies in their children. This case, however, in which both parents have the same type of inheritance is comparatively rare.

Were we to presume that we knew enough about the inheriting of normal and pathological psychic reactions, the question would arise as to which qualities we wish to multiply, which decrease by cutting the germ-orbit? We come up against the same problem in animal breeding, in which we aim by no means at the biologically most perfect animal (in that case we would only have to

MEANS OF PUNISHMENT

give nature free rein), but breed certain teratological
types, functional exaggerations which are, it is true, of
benefit to the breeder himself, but not to the animal.

But has the danger suddenly grown so enormous that
old selective mechanisms no longer suffice? Those pessi-
mistically inclined say yes. The waves of degeneration
rise higher and higher, up to the neck of civilization and
the healthy continuity of civilized peoples. Between
the unchecked growth of the inferior and the retrogression
of the gifted and healthy there is growing a biological
and thus social, catastrophe.

Apart from the horrible chronicles of the families
Kallikak, Jukes, &c., whose unscientific method of
investigation is scarcely contested to-day, there still
remains an abundance of statistical accounts which show
a great increase in the numbers of the inmates of asylums
and of the feeble-minded. Kankeleit has produced the
figures of the lunatics, epileptics and feeble-minded
looked after in the Hamburg asylums, according to which
out of every thousand of the population there were in

1877—2.31 patients, 1907—3.70 patients.
1887—3.26   ,,   1917—4.01   ,,
1897—2.90   ,,   1927—5.66   ,,

Landman quotes the following figures from the United
States. In the State sanatoria and nursing homes the
number of patients for every 100,000 of the population
was

1880— 63.7, 1910—173.0,
1890—107.6, 1929—225.9.

So, altogether, a considerable increase in the insane. The
only question which remains is whether this increase
shows an unceasing augmentation of the number of
degenerates or whether it depends on other reasons. Such

181

reasons could be the improvement and development of psychiatric diagnosis, the decreasing aversion to lunatic asylums, the increasing pressure of surroundings, and above all of life in large cities, then the increased length of life, decrease in infant mortality which counteracts natural selection and allows of a great number of psychically defective types growing up. The reason for examples like the principality Lippe: 1804—92 insane and feeble-minded, 1908—474 patients, lies in our growing knowledge of mental disorders, and not only in a growth of deficient hereditary dispositions. Although these figures, it is true, appear ominous, but yet give no quite definite information, we must look round for other material to prove the increase in invalids, defectives and weaklings, in a word, the inferior, to which a decrease in the gifted and healthy corresponds.

Burgdörfer has investigated the propagation of various social strata in Germany, and come, like Leonard Darwin before him, to the following result : —

In 1926 in the German administration there were children under fourteen years of age

	for every official generally	for every married official
Higher officials—	0.64	0.77
Average ,, —	0.83	0.95
Lower ,, —	0.95	1.08

In this phenomenon Kankeleit sees with Burgdörfer: " Uneconomic working through insufficient propagation of the bearer of the best inheritance "; with Max v. Gruber : " Reduction of the nation to a rabble."

It is dangerous to take the social position to which a person has climbed as a sure criterion of his biological or even social superiority, otherwise princes and other Cæsar-like figures would be eugenically ideal types. Every account which in some way compares the number of children in the higher and lower strata and from their disproportion comes to the conclusion of the ominous dying out of talents and fitness, suffers from this mistake.

In the question of social utility it is just the criminal psychologist who will shun an over-valuation of purely intellectual performance, for strength of will and fresh emotionality have a much greater importance for social life and man's cohesion, than pure intellect which is essentially the personal weapon of the individual in the struggle of life.

Conversely, we can safely assume that deep down where the dregs of society flow, strata have been formed which are far beneath the domesticated type of educated workman, unadapted to modern civilized life, estranged by war or its after effects and only support themselves by the primitive means of crime. It would be a serious mistake to confound with the poor part of the population these criminal or criminaloid groups which only to small extent fall within psychiatric categories and which are continually replenished by types which sink from the upper strata. The ' lower ' economic stratum shows an astonishing loyalty to the law under the most oppressive conditions, and thus gives proof that at least their social consciousness is well developed. These sporadically distributed groups of an underworld which reaches far into the upper strata cannot be comprehended in statistics.

If the problem is attacked by investigating the fertility of the inferior, then one can quote individual cases in which an unusually high fertility is evident. But the English inquiry into sterilization has, and as I think rightly, pointed out that it would be easy to put against these exceptional cases a large number of cases in which the fertility was very low, so the English report comes to the conclusion that its own investigations cannot prove that fertility is abnormally high in imbeciles nor can it be proved by the material available. In 3733 cases of defective parents which were investigated, the total number of children bred was 8841. Of these children 2001 or 22.5 per cent. had already died, a certain proof of the abnormally high mortality among the children of defectives. This question of whether mental defects have any connexion with a large number of children must be still more closely investigated.

We are kept from coming to the conclusion of 'inferiority' to which the social station of the moment leads us, by the experiences which we underwent in the European upheaval of 1917-33, and which, being partially repeated, produced a radical change of strata. The struggle which, even before the war, was waged with bitterness is better replaced by the employment of direct material, the investigation of the feeble-minded, &c.; their fertility, the frequency with which they marry, and their infant mortality. The way is shown by the last English figures regarding former pupils of schools for the mentally backward. Of 100 male and 82 female former pupils of these schools, who are now aged between 20 and 25, only 3 males married (in the ordinary population 15 to 20 would have married), and 10 females (against at least 25 marriages in the ordinary population). But, on the other hand, it is worth emphasizing that the 82 women had 11 illegitimate children, which figure is far above the average.

But if, as we must suppose, heredity plays an important part in the genesis of mental deficiencies and disorders, and if sterilization is a sure means of blocking the germinal orbit of those afflicted, then we must admit the measure to the arsenal of criminal jurisdiction.

184

MEANS OF PUNISHMENT

With all emphasis I maintain this demand which I made twenty-one years ago.

The only questions which remain are, to what extent the measure is to be applied, what are the given conditions and in what province or provinces do the counter-indications lie.

The problem of sterilization and similar interferences interests us only in as far as biological inferiority and social menace coincide. Our attention is fixed on the struggle against a social phenomenon, crime, of which corporal and mental deficiency is only one of the causal elements.

We ask, to what extent do we affect crime if, because of certain psycho-pathological symptoms, we sterilize the feeble-minded or insane?

A glance at the not very numerous statistics of the social behaviour of the insane and the feeble-minded keeps us from erroneous views. To be sure, the insane form a considerable contingent in the numbers of those who commit single, particularly exciting, crimes, such as murder, arson and bodily injuries of varying gravity. But the great majority of crimes consists of offences against property. The insane are not lacking here, but their small group is completely overshadowed by the enormous number of the not-insane.

If we rely on recent Belgian investigations, then it is neither the insane nor the feeble-minded who constitute the chief problem of diagnosis and treatment, but those defective types which Belgian praxis calls unbalanced (disequilibrés) and whose deficiency lies more in the sphere of volition, of emotional sensibility and of moral sense. These types, which can only be affected by sterilization in their coarsest forms and with the most varied diagnoses, are the kernel of the criminological problem, as is shown by the following figures taken from Vervaeck : —

On 31st December, 1931 and 1932, there were interned in the Belgian institutes for social protection,

	Men Per Cent.	Women Per Cent.
Insane (malades mentaux), - -	21	36
Feeble-minded (debiles mentaux),	31	26
Psychopaths (disequilibrés), - -	48	38

From this we could expect the sterilization of the insane and feeble-minded to have a positive but comparatively not very important influence on the course of crime. Besides, the results of the examination of 3,500,000 army recruits in America in 1916 have so shattered the hitherto existing ideas on the proportion of feeble-minded in the free population that the assertion of a close causal connexion between imbecility and crime is no longer tenable.

There are other doubtful questions which need to be elucidated before the criminologist can decide as to how far the sterilization of the insane and mentally deficient serves his purpose. In the sterilization catalogues are listed together: hereditary imbecility, schizophrenia, manic-depressive psychosis, idiopathic epilepsy, Huntington's chorea. All these disorders, however, are neither numerically equal nor do they influence social life in the same way. Of the cases of psychosis admitted for sterilization to the asylums those suffering from schizophrenia are right at the top and then after a long interval come the manic-depressives strongly represented on the feminine side.

What is also important is the age at which they were taken ill, or better, at which they were admitted, for if the germinal orbit is not blocked, before several children have been bred, it goes on. In America the average age of those admitted is 42.6 years; a figure which is admittedly forced up by those who had developed senile maladies. The groups of schizophrenia, psychopathia and mental deficiency have all the same ages of admittance of 32.2, 32.1 and 31.7 years. It is self-evident that up to this age all sorts of things can be done for propagation.

Finally, the figures of discharges and the dates of marriages of the insane and the mentally deficient are relevant to the problem. The frequency of marriage is low among schizophrenics and epileptic men, and strikingly high among manic-depressive women. An attentive praxis of sterilization should not leave these facts out of consideration.

I pass over other facts which show that biological and social selection sometimes coincide, but that they also sometimes diverge. Great artists and important scholars may be biologically deficient and in their purely social accomplishments absolutely sufficient: taking the long view, to them, as dispensers of imperishable vital impulses, belongs the title of being of the highest utility for the vitality, even the coherence of a nation. From another side the biologically superior, the cautious, the clever, the favourite, the loved, the strong-willed and corporally fit daily break through the front of law and order. They are not discovered, nor can they be convicted; they are acquitted. Still further the State which seeks a clear aim in breeding for its sterilization plans must take care not to breed out courage, though it is momentarily troublesome, and repress it with the means of penal law, for a weak and startled fear of the law is sometimes nothing but a form of degeneration which

187

is socially inconspicuous and comfortable but extremely
dangerous for the State in times of crisis.

But in the advantage of the operation ' in itself,'
there still remains to be weighed all that which could
appear as injury to the individual or the commonwealth
in a common appreciation of sterilization as a treatment.

In eugenic and criminological praxis surgical interference must not be resorted to if it should be personally
dangerous or of great consequence to the patient and if
there should be other harmless and nearly equally sure
means of ' sterilizing ' the defective. Such means would
be: eugenic education, advice on marriage, contracep-
tive instruction, forbiddal of marriage and, finally,
detention. It is clear that for just the psychically
insufficient human types only segregation would furnish
a certain means of sterilization. In direct effectiveness
surgical interference stands far and away at the top,
even when one takes into consideration the possibility
of ' recanalization.'

Most eugenists agree that vasectomy has no risk for
men. Of normal men who had been sterilized, a third
stated that the operation had not kept them one day
from their work. Ligature of the tubes and similar
operations on women are to be taken considerably more
seriously, for here, after all, the abdominal cavity must
be opened.

In view of the mild view taken by eugenists, it must
be surprising that a highly qualified expert like Reuter
has in Court called operations to close the spermatic
duct ' serious injury ' in the meaning of penal law.
Later experts have associated themselves with this severe
opinion. The Court's acceptance of the fact that it is
generally possible to restore the procreative faculty after

vasoligation, vasectomy and similar operations alone prevented the passing of a severe sentence on the surgeons; the indication was a social one, but the operative technique was exactly the same. Thus the assumption of loss of the procreative faculty was taken from the prosecution's case. This fact is eugenically and legally of equal importance.

The after-effects of the usual surgical methods of sterilization are, too, generally regarded as insignificant. But here, too, it is only with the course of years that we will arrive at reliable results.

In men interruption of spermatogenesis can be noticed at the beginning, but it seems that with continued closure of the spermatic duct the formation of semen adapts itself to the new conditions and partially recovers. A case of mechanical injury which was observed must be still more closely investigated. The authors who have investigated the operations of others or reported the results of operations resulting from their own diagnosis, differ in their judgments. The ' serious injury ' of the Austrian expert and the opinion of the Danish Court physician, Knud Sand, that in sterilization, apart from the cancellation of procreative faculty, the bodily and psychic condition remains unaltered, is an example of such a disagreement.

Intensification of sexual appetence which seems not infrequently to occur in sterilization is to be taken more seriously than local residua like alterations to the spermatic duct, indurations in the epididymis, tenderness and indurations in the testicles, relaxed suspension of the testicles, azoospermia, or at least oligospermia. Landman has already described, from P. Popenoe, the effects of such on men and women. The recent after examination of 97 cases at Graz lead to the following result :—

(1) No change of any kind in sexual life and psychic state, - - - - - -   23
(2) Increase of libido, without any bodily or psychic change, - - - - -   12
(3) No change in sexual life, with subjective improvement in bodily and psychic condition, - - - - - - -   20
(4) Intensification of sexual life and subjective improvement in bodily and psychic state,   38
(5) Diminution of sexual life and small psychical change, - - - - -   4

—

97

With the eugenic practical effect is connected an effect which cannot be socially or criminologically welcomed. If sterilization relieves the overfilled asylums, yet with intensification of sexual appetence one can say that there is increased ripeness for these institutions. Perhaps this is the reason why the English superintendents think that they would only be able to discharge 3 to 5 per cent. of the inmates if sterilization were introduced.

There remain two questions to be considered, that of psychic effect and that of intensification of appetence which immediately introduces the problem of the sterilized feeble-minded as an infectious seat of moral and bodily harm.

There is a lack of material obtained by experience, statistically sufficient and worked out with all objectivity and every means of science. It is not right to examine only ' normal women ' or, on the other hand, to put forward only the results of the examination of sterilized imbeciles. It is probable that the English are right in their opinion that in many cases of psychic disorder the indications are just against sterilization.

The question of whether the interference is voluntarily allowed or compulsorily undertaken seems material. In the one case the operation can release, as painful or oppressive experience, all those mechanisms of sickness which may follow automatically on a physiopsychic trauma.

We will come across a last objection in the question of castration directly : that of the effect of the operation on popular opinion. But none of the doubts brought forward affect the eugenic effect of sterilization. It stands secure, and nothing can shake it. The only thing to decide is whether the affected values of the individual and the generality are not likely to recom- mend the utmost care and scrupulousness to surgical sterilization.

Since Germany with the law of the 24th November, 1933, introduced the severest form of sterilization, castra- tion, for persistent offenders against morality (or those committing at least two delicts) the criminologist cannot leave these new securative means out of consideration.

It were idle to dispute as to whether castration is abstractly a preventive measure or a punishment. The history of penal law shows that practically every organ which at one time or another was regarded as the seat of the soul or life force, the head, heart, blood and phallus, has also been the object of attack of penal law. The consciously chosen expression of the German law for the proceeding ' emasculation ' which has been given a certain meaning in linguistic development and which is foreign to surgical praxis, points and works in the direction of deterrence. ' Emasculation ' is also,

191

in popular opinion, a hundred times more serious evil than the requisite main preceding punishment.

But it is not these points of dogmatic controversy which should hold us up. We are only concerned with the criminological aspect, whose treatment is all the more difficult as German law embarks on completely new ways. As far as Landman's work reproduces American legislation up to 1932, there is no prototype in the United States, the Danish law of 1st June, 1929, and the Norwegian law of 1st June, 1934, make the admissibility of a castration dependent on quite different and much more selected conditions.

Castration seeks to suppress crimes against morality. Thus, as well as the eugenic object which would also be attained by sterilization, it has criminological aims. When an individual has criminal tendencies, it is from the bodily side that these menacing tendencies are to be affected and deadened. The eugenic purpose will with certainty be obtained; all that remains to be examined are the effects on the individual and, behind the individual, the generality, its feelings and the sum of its conceptions.

The theory of intimidation presumes that every act of punishment by the State makes a deep impression on the imagination of those who come under its laws. Every sentence implies, so one says, a strong restraining suggestion which is transmitted to a great distance.

This idea is correct in that from the State's punitive activity psychic rays spread in all directions; here their interference is restraining, there they hasten the emotional sequence. The punitory state is every minute confronted with the very difficult problem of how it is to bring its measures of combating crime into harmony with its task of being a model, and as a model of behaviour how it is to force powerful, automatically effective suggestions on the masses. Here the difficulties occasioned by castration as a State measure are unmistakable. The whole circle of conceptions surrounding sexuality is in itself shaken. We rightly endeavour to restore a portion of their ancient strength to those things which are crowned by the idea of motherhood. It is dangerous to weaken the primarily useful suggestion of inviolability and sanctity with measures of secondary utility. These effects do not take place immediately nor can they be clearly recognized in the course of a few years. They will be the subject of an endless dispute between the supporters and opponents of deterrence, a dispute which may only be decided in historical retrospect. Sooner, but also only after a period of years, we will have at our disposal the experiences gained from operative interference on individuals.

Now we can only say that we are completely without material. But what we do not have and what we need are closely watched results on people who have been castrated by order of the criminal court, that is to say, *manu militari*, and who have had to come to a fresh understanding with free life. Investigations like those of Lange are unquestionably of great value: but his 179 wound-castrated are as little to be compared with those condemned to emasculation, with reference to the personal experience of castration, as patients who, for some reason or other, have castrated themselves or had themselves operated on. Soldiers are psychically and corporally a different material from the offender against morality, their mutilation arouses sympathy and leads to a pension, while for the castrated offender against morality there waits an entirely different reception which is partly the result of externally perceptible change in his corporeality, but above all of a reaction of aversion on the part of the population.

Kopp has reported on the examination of 40 sexual offenders from the Zurich Clinic, made by A. W. Hackfield. Knud Sand has advanced an opinion on the Danish observations; and there is also the work of Johannes Lange and a collection of observations made in the Basle Surgical Clinic published by Ch. Wolf. The results are so inconsistent because Hackfield examined a very polymorphous group of perverse psychopaths, homosexuals, insane, and finally menstrually excited or sexually unprincipled women. Knud Sand had before him feeble-minded, ' weak-headed ' and psychopathic castrated persons, Lange chiefly war-wounded, and C. H. Wolf examined patients of the surgical clinic. Of the 74 people who constituted the Danish material, there were 35 homosexuals, four were guilty of incest or sodomy. This whole group is, however, according to the German law exempt from castration.

As well as other results there without doubt occur disorders of perseverance and elasticity, weakened interest loosens important life relations, an effect which is known in animal breeding. Potence and libido-maintenance are differently judged. Lange's 81 wound-castrated gave the following results:—

Potence immediately extinguished - -	44
Potence maintained - - - - -	20
Potence slowly extinguished - - - -	17

Hackfield saw no operative success either in reference to psychic derangement or tendency to offences against morality, especially in the case of the castrated insane. Knud Sand's judgment is more favourable; he was unable to establish actual sexual practices in any of the castrated, but, it is true, occasional suspicious interest for sexual objects and the introduction of erotic connexes. Although one could say that in bodily symptoms many castrated have had no reason to ' complain,' yet matters are quite different as far as sexual expression is concerned. Of 59 male patients, at the time of the operation only 13 were at liberty, all the others were interned in institutions, that is to say, they had an explainable interest in keeping possible sexual impulses secret or in denying them.

In view of these uncertainties and secondary effects, the interference, which is pregnant with results, would nevertheless be indicated, if other available preventives had failed; that is to say, imprisonment as well as pure detaining measures, and, in certain circumstances also castration on medical grounds, must have proved unfit to neutralize the dangerous tendencies of the offender. Here we leave the eugenic object which could be obtained by simple sterilization purposely out of consideration.

In Germany there were condemned for offences and crimes against morality, out of every 100,000 old enough to be punished—

1882-91—22	1910—31	1924—27	1928—27
1895—29	1913—33	1925—34	1929—27
1900—29	1921—22	1926—34	1930—27·2
1905—32	1923—20	1927—31	1931—25·7

When we consider that there has been considerable increase on the number of legal dispositions in 1900, the inference is that the level of offences against morality is under that of 1900 and probably under that of the initial date in our statistics. Thus one cannot speak of a complete failure of the old repressive mechanisms. Admittedly, just this type of crime is particularly dependent on the actual moral level and also on the partner's consent with whom denunciation and prosecution rests.

A series of facts advise the criminologist to prefer to save the great, developable idea of eugenics from setbacks by trying to obtain for the time being experiences through voluntary or quasi-voluntary sterilization and medico-socially indicated castration. Further development depends on their results, and not on any theoretical speculation. An inexperienced law-giver continues to be a speculative theorist.

We recognized the magic and religious origin of the death penalty. The purpose of whipping, too, was at first not the infliction of pain. The ritual of the execution in many mediæval towns, like Speier, displays a close resemblance between the later punitive act and the very ancient magic agency of ' knocking off.' Knocked off are all kinds of evil: illness, insanity, fatigue, fault and wickedness.

Just so castration can be reduced to a stratum of older notions. Past times believed all male force and all criminal activity concentrated in the testicles. Removing the testicles signified deliverance from a source of wicked ideas and malicious forces. Even the severed member was deemed so pernicious that the testicles of the self-emasculating priests of Attis were buried, so to speak, alive. The same precautions were taken in the mediæval criminal practice.

4. Deportation

Although it incorporates a number of new elements, deportation is allied to imprisonment, but also borders on capital punishment, and if one looks closer into it, one may observe that deportation at the time of the

Roman emperors in England, France and Russia did not always necessarily take the form of a mitigated infliction of the death penalty.

In ancient Rome the practice of deportation spread when the Stoic teaching of the nullity of life, combined with a real disinclination for life, internally debilitated the death penalty and at the same time fear taught the emperors to avoid indiscriminate and visible exercise of the death penalty on persons from whose family or class with its sentiment of interdependence an avenger might come.

The emperor had to see that by executing individuals he did not further decimate the upper classes on whose intermediate support his authority depended. Every execution alienated an entire group of relations or friends even when they did not resort to direct attack.

In a famous but little known conversation with Augustus, Livia expressed the following idea which shows a very fine feminine instinct. " For that reason, solitude is hazardous, equally hazardous is society, it is dangerous to have no guards, but most dangerous are the guards themselves. Our enemies will be fatal to us, more fatal our friends, and we must call them friends, however little they are such . . . The worst is that we must take strong measures against such as lie in wait for us." This could have been written by Machiavelli; and though it may perhaps have not been said but taken by the historian from Court gossip, still that does not alter its profound wisdom.

Holtzendorff thinks that this development was occasioned by the gradually rising distinction between *persones honestiores* and *humiliores*, but one could equally well think that the division into two personal fields of punishment was brought about by the different methods

197

of treating strata which seemed dangerous or harmless to the emperor. At any rate, for the Roman senator with his exaggerated sensitiveness, his propensity to comfort and his complete dependence on the help of paid servants, deportation to one of the most notorious islands, Gyarus, Seriphos, Amoyos, Patmos, Kossura, Skyros, Skiathos, Donusa, and other islands of the Ægean Sea, was a far severer punishment than taking poison or the gentle death in a hot bath with a cut artery. The tiny, comfortless islands near Italy and Sicily of which we know from the unhappy history of the family of the first emperor (Pandataria, Planasia, Ponza, Trimerus) were far more dangerous for the deported person than more distant islands, because the anger of the sovereign took quicker effect here and the control was sharper.

We know more about two such devil's islands, Gyarus enjoyed the worst reputation; Juvenal compares banishment to Gyarus to the death penalty. When in the reign of Tiberius it was moved in the Senate to inflict the horrible punishment for patricide on Serenus, the emperor interceded; then when Gallus Asinius further moved that Serenus be banished to Gyarus or Dunusa, the emperor again exercised his veto. One island like the other suffered from a shortage of water, and if one left a person his life, one must also afford him the possibility of keeping body and soul together. Gyarus, a small island in the northern group of the Cyclades, lay about 19 kilometres distant from the larger island. The island was rocky, desolate, arid and had no harbour. Strabo quotes a verse from Arabus, according to which the pregnant Latona was given the island of Delos as a resting-place, otherwise she must repose on the miserable Gyarus. There are all sorts of stories about these islands; that the inhabitants had had to flee from a plague of mice or a swarm of locusts. It was Gyarus that Tiberius, who knew the islands of the Ægean, called barren and uninhabitable during the trial of Serenus.

Corsica, as an island for deportation, is brought closer to us by Seneca's banishment and his moving plaint. Strabo only softens the dark picture of the island a little: "Kyrnos is called Corsica by the Romans; it is sparsely inhabited because it is rugged and most parts are completely inaccessible, so that the inhabitants of the mountains, who live from brigandage, are wilder than the animals. Whenever the Roman armies attacked them and stormed their strongholds, taking a large number of prisoners, one could see from the slaves who were taken to Rome how clearly their animal and bestial nature was revealed. They could either no longer bear to live or, if they continued alive, they so angered their purchasers by their apathy and stupidity that, even though they had only paid a low price, they yet regretted their purchase."

Deportation was regularly accompanied by confiscation of property and loss of civic rights. Often there were degrees of severity as to the place to which one was deported, varying from very severe to mild. Sometimes, too, the banished were killed by order of the emperor during transit to the place of banishment. In comparison to other means of punishment deportation allowed of an individual treatment. Naxos, Cyprus, Rhodes and Crete were mild places of banishment. Tiberius in his voluntary self-banishment had withdrawn to Rhodes which was famous for its good climate, when he fell victim to a depressive attack.

The rare cases of deportation to an oasis with a specially dangerous climate make us think of the attempts at large-scale deportation which the nations with great

199

colonial possessions made a long time afterwards and are partly still making to-day. Here, too, it was not considerations of criminal law but economic or political necessities which made the new methods necessary. One cannot say that deportation has deviated much from being a bloodless form of capital punishment since the time of the Roman emperors. At the most, in those places where an economic effect, the provision of labour, was aimed at, the decision between physical destruction and aspired gain was made in favour of strong advantages and the humaneness which went with them.

English deportation followed the discovery of a new continent in the west which suddenly offered an immense economic object which could only be exploited by manual labour. The first rudimentary laws on deportation date from 1597; they concerned beggars and tramps. In 1606 the Virginia Company was founded by James I. And after 1618 the deportation of prisoners was a regular method of inflicting punishment. The importation of black labour gave the first serious blow to the commercial heart of deportation, and when war broke out between the American colonies and the mother country, the doors were automatically shut against the importation of prisoners (about 1779). Then came the great Australian experiment (beginning 1787) with far more than 100,000 condemned people of whom some were killed on the voyage out, some in Australia itself, and some saved from the fate of rotting in unhealthy hulks or insupportable prisons, were brought to a new and better life, if there was any spark at all capable of development in them. When the opposition of voluntary emigrants grew and in 1867 the last transports had left, the great experiment in infliction of punishment, in spite of many mistakes, could not be called a failure; the necessity of falling back on the labour of the deported, where it was employable, had in Australia never allowed of deportation degenerating into safe custody with gradually resulting death. Even the climatic conditions, as it was a question of an aspiring, productive colony, were never studiedly bad. When at the beginning of the second-third of the nineteenth century the spread of machinery led to much unrest and unemployment, there were many bitter comparisons made between the lot of the free English workmen and that of the deported; the favourable position of the deported, said a governor of Van Diemen's Land, will all too easily lead the lower classes to the conclusion of how unprofitable an honest life is and how extraordinarily advantageous depravity.

Russian deportation would have been much more appreciated in its criminological and positive significance had the administration's arrangements for dispatching the prisoners not discredited the whole idea. It is well known that under Friedrich Wilhelm III of Prussia experiments were made with deporting Prussian criminals to Siberia.

French transportation (together with forced labour) and relegation show all the infirmities of deportation, a bad climate (tropics), predominance of purely securative methods, above all in Guayana, very high mortality and slight feasibility of productive work.

The claims of improved execution are best developed in complete antithesis to the French fashioning of the institution of deportation. In this we must make a sharp distinction between two functions; securative detention in some territory far from the homeland, such as an island, and the reformative effect which may result from a sum of negative and positive factors, from the removal from injurious influences of the home *milieu*, from the application of climatic forces which could be portioned out to excite or restrain, further, from tasks given to the surplus force, enterprise, sometimes, too, desire for power, of the condemned, in indulging in which he gradually fits himself into a social order. In deportation there also disappear those depressing influences which at home often force the previously convicted back into the world of crime.

Purely tropical countries are little suited to deportation on a large scale; they are equally dangerous to the superintendents or pedagogues and the condemned. I do not see why civilized States make agreements about white-slave traffic, drugs and every other conceivable thing, but the deportation of elements capable of reform, especially youthful elements, to certain unused territories could not be arranged without changing their constitutional laws. Just as the police follow mutual, international interests, so there are mutualities in the executing of corrections.

And the confirmed criminal, too, will experience the safest custody in an island institution, whose insuperable wall is the sea.

5. IMPRISONMENT

The restriction of the freedom of movement has developed out of three or four quite primitive forms of impediment, the pit, the stake, the cage and the fetter. It was only later that a human guard was added and then mostly as an aggravation.

The pit which was used since earliest times as well and granary and then also as dwelling, was the chief means of mastering powerful animals, as it still is in the jungle. One could only catch men and animals in pits because these deep holes kept them securely till hunger or exhaustion overcame them. In the Vedic belief Hell is a deep pit into which He who keeps order throws the disobedient. Many later types of prison have kept the form of a pit, like the Roman *carcer Mamertinus*, which must have been a well shaft, the underground prison into which the guilty Vestal was shut alive and the castle dungeons of our Middle Ages. The prisoner was let down from above, just as originally the person was thrown in or fell in.

The original form of imprisonment was, among the Vedic Arians a firmly planted stake to which the delinquent was bound with cords; as well as the stake the Indians also used a block. The cage is still to be seen in old German towns like Quedlinburg or Münster. A cage was the punishment of shrewish women (the ' Beisskatze ' of Goslar, &c.).

Fettering was a further method of hindering freedom of movement and, lastly, there comes the guard of armed men who prevent flight. One can see in the Greek words for prison, Δεσμωτηριον and φυλακή, to which the Latin *carcer* and *custodia* exactly correspond, their derivation from ' fettering ' and ' confinement by means of guards.'

Economic or other very practical considerations were at the bottom of such an expensive and laborious method as the restriction of freedom. One could only decide to imprison if the advantages of letting the person live made up for the inconvenience of shutting him up, feeding and guarding him. Such a factor was his power of working. Thus the slave kennel and with it the gladiatorial school was one of the original forms of the prison. Imprisonment during trial and imprisonment for debt equally necessitated guaranteed arrest. If the carrying out of the death sentence was continually postponed, imprisonment for life followed of itself. When

PUNISHMENT

Mommsen says that neither the Republic nor the age of the emperors used public imprisonment as a punishment, he relies on the sources which declare such a praxis to be legally inadmissible. The actual praxis will often have appeared different.

The imprisonment of the old German law was thralldom. Prison is very seldom mentioned. " In spite of the regulation," writes Wilda, " that each official had to see to the provision of suitable prisons, there was even later in Germanic countries a complete lack of places for keeping the accused and especially the convicted." When there was scarcely anything, there also a further development could not take place.

In the Middle Ages matters only took most hesitant steps forward. Life was hard and difficult and prison seemed to lack a deterrent effect. The cost was high; banishment from the city a quicker and cheaper method. Prisoners awaiting trial were confined in a tower, where also were the torture chambers. The next development was the debtor's dungeon and, finally, a strong prison for the small criminal fry. Imprisonment for life was very exceptional and mostly an act of grace or prudence. The large cities had a number of the most different prisons. It was a return to the oldest forms of imprisonment when in Nürnberg the condemned person was fastened to a bench or attached by a chain to a wall in his house. The galleys which since the seventeenth century had seriously competed with capital punishment among all great seafaring nations, were floating prisons. According to an ordnance made by Queen Elizabeth in 1602, all condemned persons except those guilty of murder, rape and burglary, were not to be executed but sent to the galleys. The experiment was also made of sending the Nürnberg criminals to the Genoese galleys and lasted without much profit till 1708. We know of similar experiments made by Switzerland and Augsburg. According to Osenbrüggen, Lucerne had once even put a galley on the lake.

When in the early Middle Ages the monasteries expanded, the idea of imprisonment was probably that clerics who had incurred punishment should not be kept publicly and to the shame of the whole priesthood, but secured and out of sight. The idea of imprisonment which had gained ground through the experiments in large-scale deportation and the punishment of being sent to the galleys, received a quickening impulse from this side. The large cities had already introduced compulsory labour in the open air on the Roman pattern for the lesser criminal. In the first convict prisons of Amsterdam, Bremen, Hamburg and Lubeck the scene of this compulsory labour was shifted indoors. When the fight against capital punishment started with the age of enlightenment, the idea of prevention awoke, and mercantilistic ideas of an improved utilization of human strength came in; imprisonment had reached that point in its development where it must automatically take over the functions of capital and corporal punishment. To begin with, it retained fettering and beating, often even the pit character of the underground dungeons, but then slowly threw off the useless remnants of earlier strata of development. It became the punishment of the new criminal law, underwent several changes, which completely altered its character and led from the bogy house of San Michele over the Eastern Penitentiary and Auburn to modern appropriate punishments which are still seeking the ultimate and strongest purport.

Right up to the present day imprisonment has been

corporal punishment. It holds the prisoner fast within the prison walls and directs its excruciating impressions against his body and soul. If we could get a close idea of the mortality among prisoners in the eighteenth and the first half of the nineteenth centuries, we should realize that the convict prison was a kind of capital punishment spread over a lengthy period; only its execution was withdrawn from public gaze and put behind high walls. In the convict prison the conditions necessary to life were consciously deteriorated to such an extent that everyone who was not bodily and psychically quite robust must succumb to the sum of these artificial injuries.

Imprisonment in that rough age was consciously concentrated partly on physical destruction and partly on energetic deterrence. It ruined the prisoner's health and intellect. But this result was not dangerous to the peace of the generality, because he was kept in custody for many years, often for as long as he lived, and only left the prison on a bier or as a complete wreck.

For this exterior reason there were in the beginning no problems of imprisonment. There was extravagance with human life, waste of the population's compassion, but in the simplest mechanical sense, the original system must be called effective.

Difficulties first arose when, with the philosophic demand for a proportionality between crime and punishment, very long or life-long imprisonment began to fall into disuse. Up till now the pernicious results of an imprisonment which concentrated on the infliction of pain had remained confined to the prison and thus isolated, but now the prisoner returned sooner or later, according to the gravity of his crime, to freedom. He came back with his power of working broken and his will to work destroyed, often completely poisoned by the condensed human depravity into which he had been thrust; his picture of the world obscured; and if he wished, perfect in the technique of committing crimes and securing himself against pursuit. Everything which had been bad or diseased, bent or weak in this man, now returned intensified into the outside world, and indeed an outside world which had become much more difficult for the discharged prisoner. It was not surprising that this was the beginning of the age of relapse, of legislative perplexity and of a quick, excited change of theories and methods of treatment.

One saw clearly that the aggregation of people who were partly true criminals and partly those who had committed punishable actions under the pressure of their unfavourable surroundings, must lead to a levelling of the collective psychic *niveau* and that this assimilation could only be in the direction of a sinking of the moral level. It was recognized that such a dangerous result could perhaps be put up with when the punishments were very long, but that the gravest inconvenience would result if the term of imprisonment were to become shorter and shorter and the punished returned more and more quickly to the slippery ground of freedom.

The process of shortening the term of imprisonment goes irresistibly forward in every civilized country; occasional outbreaks of a sudden prolongation, such as were attempted in the New York Baumes Laws, were not lasting. The similar European enactments are discoloured by frequent general pardons of the ruling party's adherents and are beside the question.

The tempo and scope of this occurrence are to be seen

from the following table of the official figures for Austria.

Average of the years	Percentage of convictions to imprisonment for a term of					
	up to 1 month	1 to 3 months	3 to 6 months	6 to 12 months	1 to 5 years	5 and more years
1882-1890	6	34	26	16	16	2
1901-1910	14	34	28	13	10	1
1924-1925	22	43	20	9	6	0.3

These figures are in respect of those who suffered imprisonment for an infringement of the law. In the years 1924-25 out of 100 offenders imprisoned 65 got under 3 months and 85 under 6 months. These short terms of imprisonment have no securative function; the period is otherwise much too short to allow of an earnest educative effect or even of only a training for a profession. But this period is also quite sufficient to infect the condemned with the seeds of moral contagion and to discharge them into liberty as ' previously convicted ' after the comparatively well-equipped buildings and relatively good treatment have robbed them of their fear of prison.

Those jails, which have not yet quite disappeared and whose only difference from the cages of the zoological gardens is that the modern zoo is infinitely more friendly and humane in its accommodation, were built with the object of deterrence.

The result of this accentuated and desired deterrent effect was that the criminal was pictured as a terrible person. After treatment by the State he seemed to be chronically extremely dangerous and only tameable by brutal methods. True, this picture only corresponded to reality for a small group of criminal types; but as the result of its daily presentation it ate its way into the imagination and the emotions of the masses and rebounded on the criminal in aggressive forms when, as now with the shortened terms of imprisonment, the prisoners did not die off in prison but poured back into freedom.

This fear which is in all our blood was blind and summary and made no fine distinctions. It embraced the prisoners, not the criminals, and became a new unsuspected means of relapse. For this apprehension of the punished closed to him the entrance to a situation, to a sociable supporting circle; it provided a never-failing means of injuring the morbidly developed sensitivity there is in many people who have been in prison and of throwing them back into a world where those unfavourable values were not current, into the world of neglect and crime.

Thus the ever-shortening term of imprisonment has also brought the great crisis of prison. The corporal punishment of confinement, fettering, beating, bad nourishment and lack of light was dead. But even imprisonment as a punishment had run itself out. Like an organic being which does not want to perish and whose cell complex has only one possibility of resisting death, that of dividing itself up, so, too, has imprisonment become ripe for that division which will assure its continued existence in two quite distinct forms. Imprisonment divides into educative punishment which has an entirely different object, but borrows the external means of confinement as a frame for permanent educative interference. The other half which separates itself from imprisonment is preventative detention. Here we do not wish to punish, but we must put the immutably or provisionally unaffected by efforts to cure or educate, in a safe place, by confining them. In both cases we deprive them of their freedom but fill the gap with entirely different purports. In neither case is ' punishment ' in its former sense of beating, meagre fare and darkened cell our intention, but causal attack on lawbreakers and, where this possibility is still denied us, isolation until such time as the confined is no longer a danger to himself or to us.

6. Preventative Detention

The death penalty had the effect of giving security, as had many severe corporal punishments, such as piercing out the eyes, cutting the hands off, and as had also the confinement of a dangerous lunatic. Long imprisonments, the aim of whose term was not to give security but only corresponded to the seriousness of the deed and was to increase the intensity of the punishment, had the not directly aimed at secondary effect of keeping the criminal for a long time away from the outside world, its difficulties and too powerful temptations.

In this period the convicted person was also unable to obtain a sexual partner. He was bloodlessly sterilized. In every case in which the criminal died in prison or left it as a harmless invalid, the propagation of inferior seed was also interrupted. With a period of long, retaliatory punishment the criminal could propagate very much less and thus neither multiply nor disseminate the social danger contained in his anti-social personality.

It was thus one of the greatest ideas of modern criminology—and with this idea the name of Carl Stooss is for ever associated—to divide imprisonment, in which the useful and injurious lay side by side, into its, if I may say so, chemical components. The old method of

210

long term, and so called severe imprisonment which, owing to the length of the punishment, amounted to infliction of pain and intimidation, had in judicial praxis proved a fiasco. To this alienation contributed modern man's increased sensitivity to pain, increased sympathy with his suffering fellow-creatures and the removal of pain by means of medicine's newly discovered anæsthetics.

Short-term infliction of pain, as we learn from experience, is only in a small number of cases suited to displace deeply rooted criminal tendencies. Here the disadvantages preponderated. In those cases where pressure of surroundings had forced the deed out of a relatively social disposition, above all in cases of emergency delicts—emergency in its broadest sense as over-average external coercion—pain, which only affected the fallible person, was directed against the wrong point of attack, not always without effect, but unnecessarily destructive, and so was no clean selective method.

In the division of the old, long imprisonment into an ineffective part and a remnant of effectiveness, the long term with its energetic securative function remained. This detention over a period of years came into consideration for the most different categories of criminals who were insensitive to punishment. In the case of the insane criminal, pure custody had to be combined with attempted curative treatment. Also in the case of the mentally inferior, as well as being subjected to preventative detention, he could be partly educationally influenced and partly helped medically. To this group belong drug addicts, above all drunkards. There remains one last large group of criminals who were insensitive to punishment and for whom the ineffective means of a mild or severe punishment thus did not come into consideration at all.

PUNISHMENT

This consists of those people whom in a purely symptomatic light one calls backsliders, and who as a rule are considered a homogenous block and who yet fall into two fundamentally different strata; the one, those people whose surroundings remain always the same, similarly oppressive, prejudicial and crimogenous; here a relapse only means that a mediocre disposition always responds to a constant destructive impulse with the same reaction. There are no considerable reserves of strength which can be mobilized in the corporeality and psychic constitution of the man and which could be drawn out by such means as punishment or education. The surroundings remain constant and the relapse is the social expression of this relation between forces, which no causal dislocation has destroyed.

On the other side are the real backsliders. Here a pronouncedly criminal disposition reacts to the most varied forms of claims made on it by its surroundings, to the slightest impulse as to the heaviest shock, in constantly renewed criminal actions. For such individuals punishment has usually lost its effect. The slight so-called gravity of the act is frequently no longer able to establish the necessity for retaliation which is the hypothesis for a punishment of long duration. In this dilemma between heightened need for protection of the generality and weakened emotionality or reactivity, the way out is alone provided by the method which avoids inflicting pain and introduces securative length of duration of the treatment. The backslider is mechanically separated from the possibility of backsliding for a number of years, or better, till an alteration occurs in the fixed ratio between disposition and surroundings, which can result from the most different grounds.

The question of preventative detention depends on two

MEANS OF PUNISHMENT

hypotheses. The psychiater will tell us who is mentally disordered. The mentally inferior will coincide to a large extent with the real backslider; but the question as to who is such a real persistent offender will have to be determined by criminology. The time is imminent when the separation of exogenous and endogenous backsliding will be a scientific task.

The second question concerns the nature of the technique in treatment. When we remember that securative custody is a question of the longest and most frictionless detention possible and nothing further, then we realize that we lack to-day any experience as to how such a securative detention should be undertaken.

As well as the confinement, there is the task of continually watching the human material in custody, observing changes in bodily and psychic structure which the most different moments and developments can bring about, of correcting wrong diagnoses of true backsliding which will always occur owing to the exceptional difficulty of making a decision, of evaporating the material entrusted to us away to an assured and firm residue by means of an even keener process of selection.

I believe that we will still have surprises from a preventative detention which is cleverly determined and carried out with understanding. It will be seen that many prisons and many methods of punishment have more encouraged than hindered relapse. By that I do not mean the last fact of backsliding, but those hypotheses of being able to relapse which lie in weakening of the will, loss of real work, the crippling or morbid exaggeration of self-reliance, in the illusory falsification of position in relation to the real world, in the extortions of deeply rooted perversions of sexual life. I think that later development will again divide the protective insti-

213

tutions into two entirely different institutions: the one will have nothing but detention to do. In the other the absence of interference afforded by passive custody will give rise to new experiences, surprising effects of the action of age, of seasonable influences, climatic factors, the removal of destructive impulses of a physiological kind (undernourishment, over-exhaustion, sexual excesses, psychic affliction). These securative institutions will be our great new laboratory for constructing new, active, methods of treatment.

Preventative detention will give us yet another last surprise. We believe in the deterrent effect of punishment, because we assume that a considerable portion of offenders are caught. The real offender has a quite different opinion. He knows from his own experience that the State—*cum grano salis*—is in spite of all its efforts as blind as Polyphemus. After a long series of successful crimes there follows a professional accident, arrest and often, too, there does not. "Just from the judges," I have said elsewhere, "who go about their task with deep earnestness, few will realize how very much the real criminal plays with them, how superior they feel to the judge, how deeply they, freed of secret self-reproach, scornfully see into the judge's human weaknesses, how they triumphantly enjoy their wild life, compared with the laborious existence of the worthy, badly paid official —in spite of every punishment of the convict prison. There would be infinitely more complaining, there would be more suicides and more attacks on officials if the most dangerous criminals did not present this counter reckoning to themselves and savour it thoroughly.

The preventative detention prison will really teach the true criminal to shudder; not because it uses to guard

him the 'energetic' means, which both coarsen and
stupefy, but because it lasts as long as 'its purpose
requires.' A careful study of personality will, at any
rate, partially lighten that dark space which was filled
by the activities of undiscovered criminals, and by
elastic extension of the time of custody will make good
many a loss of our insufficiency. Known in his personality, the criminal will be identified as by an infallible
finger-print, and, subsequently called to account for his
general dangerousness, if one may use the expression.

On the other hand, there will be no great difficulty
in transferring the chronically criminal, but passive,
condemned person to milder and more productive forms
of custody, and in making up quickly for mistakes in
the difficult question of his persistence and dangerousness
for public safety. Only one further danger threatens
preventative detention; the theoretical doubt-occasioned
double-trackedness of deterrent punishment and detention. This duality, which frightens the judge away
from custody and forces him back towards punishment, is
a truly devilish invention; it destroys the scientific results
of fifty years by a pseudo-concession. We must direct all
our strength against it.

7. THE FINE

The Germanic law's compensation for injury, whether
it were mulct (pena) or weregild (satisfacio) has disappeared from our system of fines. There was in it a
touch of self-humiliation which appeased the revengeful-
ness of the injured, quite apart from the fact that weregild sought out and attacked the weakest point in the
injured's psychology. The punishing, even severely
punishing part of this solution of the conflict can only be
understood in the light of one trait of the Germanic

character, its obstinate inflexibility. In the Germanic law there appears no surrender of property or fine paid to a deity's temple treasure as in Greece or Rome. Still later, public fines could in Rome be allotted to the Treasury or the funds of a temple, but even in ancient laws an undertone of moral censure went with it, just which is wanting in fines to-day.

The early Middle Ages kept the claims of State and injured completely separate. Both demands could in the course of time be satisfied with money or certain natural products. Then the injured's title to compensation grew less and less and was slowly absorbed by the mulct which went to the State. The rights of the injured were slowly absorbed into the sphere of civil law; in the Basle of the Middle Ages the payment of a fine by the condemned person in certain delicts by no means released him from the necessity of making good the damage. Thus there could be three payments one after another: a fine paid to the court, compensation to the injured party and reparation of the damage. This separation is still preserved in valid German law in two groups of offences, which provide for separate fine and payment of compensation; at any rate a fine (Busse) does away with any legal claim to reparation of damage. This duality has already disappeared from the bills of German penal codes and with it consideration of the injured party and his non-material interests.

This separation of two functions is a serious defect in the modern system of fines which only go to the State, while the injured party suffers all the hardships of the civil process. But consideration for the injured party is here all the more requisite, the milder the fine seems according to our conception and the less it satisfies the victim's need of reaction. On the other hand, the State's allocation of the fine to itself, like in Rome under the emperors, contains the temptation to exaggerate its authority to punish. In face of the State's financial needs the principle of opportunity, which was introduced for good reasons, fails, for the State does not consider it opportune to renounce the receipt of money.

For this reason one will continually have to insist on introducing the question of compensation into criminal procedure, not for reasons of economy in procedure only, but in order to conciliate the victim with the State's " bloodless " system of punishing. In many cases payment to the injured party will have a stronger inner punishment value than the payment of a sum to the neutral State. In Germany there is the tendency to remove the question of compensation more and more from criminal procedure, palpably in the desire to avoid representation of the injured party along with the public prosecution. But I think that an examination of the question of damage would enable the punishment to be more justly apportioned and the perpetrator to be judged more in the light of psychology. Certainly the material and non-material damage caused belongs to the ' merited consequences of the deed,' which are mentioned in the Bill of a German penal code; as further according to this Bill the court shall take into consideration the personal and economic circumstances of the perpetrator at the time of the deed and of his being finally sentenced, the careful determination of the general grounds on which the punishment was apportioned would already comprise every real base of claim to compensation.

The psychology of fines is a very confused province. The fine varies subjectively according to a very variable criterion, the punished's sensibility in terms of the money he possesses. Objectively, the effect must fluctuate according to the means of the condemned. Both points of view have only a slight connexion, or no connexion at all, with the tendencies which decided the perpetrator on the delict. Compared with great, lasting aims of punishment, cure or education, fines have only a slight effect, because they are directed in no way against the person's natural disposition, but only against external aids in life, accessories foreign to his personality, that is his property.

In those cases where the fine meets with real sensitiveness as in the case of the constitutionally miserly, maniac-hoarders, it is the ideal punishment, having no unfavourable secondary effects, not involving cooping up with psychically infectious persons, or considerable expense in infliction and without those moral secondary oscillations which make imprisonment so lifelong and so impossible to overlook in its effects.

Against this advantage there is a great disadvantage. A person who can be affected by a fine can easily escape the punishment by realizing his seizable wealth. It is much more difficult to arrest nimble money than a corporal person, for the flight of money has at its disposal many forms of transport which are difficult legally to prevent. The transformation into imprisonment, however, become less and less accomplishable with the magnitude of the sum, because the duration of the substitute imprisonment brings the whole insufficiency of this stopgap method into the limelight and because in the case of large fines the question of ability to pay meets with considerable doubt. Thus in the practice of legal life large fines turn against themselves. Of those persons fined Rm 10,000 and more, according to the statistical appendix to the German Bill, in 1925 and 1926, only 5 per cent. to 6 per cent. fulfilled their obligations. How the law gets itself out of this dilemma, we do not learn.

It is true that even imprisonment of equal duration is intrinsically not the same punishment for two different people; but imprisonment interferes with the elementary necessities of man, which everywhere are repeated in one form or another. The fine, however, is directed against one of man's capacities, which admits of the most violent variation. Moreover, criminal punishment is, generally speaking, a means of selection by the State for poor people. But just in the case of poor people the fine is hindered in its application. Think only of the great European social sickness of unemployment. On the one hand the State pays a dole to the unemployed who is without means, on the other hand the same State demands an amount which narrows the life scope of the poor till it becomes intolerable. If the condemned does not pay, then undesired substitute forms come into action; if he pays, then the resulting want will easily impel him to criminal actions, which are to fill the economic vacuum which the State's proceedings have caused.

One could say that fining the rich, even a fine considered high by the judge, is as different from fining the poor, as a punishment of five years' imprisonment would be for a person who lived one thousand years and for one who lived fifty. Theoretically the laws always demand proportionality of income and amount of fine, but in practice this elastic assimilation is never reached. To lose that illusion we only need to look at the percentages of the amounts of individual fines.

The percentages of the amounts of the fines in 1911 for Germany were—

				per cent.
6	marks and less,	-	-	28.4
7 to 10	,,	-	-	18.7
11 to 15	,,	-	-	10.2
16 to 30	,,	-	-	27.9
31 to 60	,,	-	-	10.5
61 to 100	,,	-	-	2.8
101 to 150	,, .	-	-	0.7
151 to 300	,,	-	-	0.6
301 to 600	,,	-	-	0.2
601	marks and more,	-	-	0.05

According to this, fines of over 60 marks play only an unimportant part. This modesty can again be observed in an experiment which was made in Germany. Since 1924 the province in which fines can be inflicted has, with a certain large-scale audacity, been extended by replacing an incurred imprisonment of less than three months for minor offences with a fine, " if the object of the punishment can be attained by means of a fine " (§27b St GB.). The consideration of the, to be sure, simplified new statistics of fines, which already embraces the great extension of the use of fines, shows that in comparison to the earlier statistics there has been no essential alteration. The substitution of a fine for imprisonment moves within the slight limits of 1-100 marks and only occasionally goes above this level.

The numbers of the persons condemned for crimes or offences against the laws of the Reich to fines is divided among the individual categories in the following manner :—

MEANS OF PUNISHMENT

							1926
Amounts of less than 20 marks	-	-	44.5
From 20 up to 100 marks -	-	-	47.9
,, 100 ,, 300 ,,	-	-	-	6.3
,, 300 ,, 1,000 ,,	-	-	-	1.0
,, 1000 ,, 10,000 ,,	-	-	-	0.2
Over 10,000 - - -	-	-	-	0.05

Of 100 known fines in 1926, 13.3 were incurred imprisonment of under three months. Here results the following division of the individual categories of punishment, which must really be very different from the usual fine—

						1926
Amounts of 20 marks and less	-	-	32.7
,, 20 ,, up to 100 marks	56.2
,, 100 ,, ,, 300 ,,	9.5
,, 300 ,, ,, 1000 ,,	1.4
,, 1000 ,, ,, 10,000 ,,	0.2
Over 10,000 marks - - -	-	-	0.01

92.4 per cent. of all fines and 88.9 per cent. of transformed imprisonments are of less than 100 marks. If we consider with what pertinacity one once clung to the necessity of capital punishment for offences against property and then the necessity of imprisonment, and when we learn that in 1927 50.9 of all the sentences for simple theft in Germany took the form of fines, then we must admit that human convictions are subject to considerable changes and will continue to be so. In spite of the fact that in 66.4 per cent. of the convictions for dangerous bodily injury, the German courts to-day (1927) allow of the transmutation of incurred imprisonment into a fine, the fines have not gone considerably above the 100-mark level.

The advance of fines is a surprising phenomenon. It indicates the admission of our helplessness, for obviously there is wanting a method of punishment, which works sensitively and yet is as innocuous as possible, between imprisonment and complete absence of punishment. This vacuum is temporarily filled by the fine.

The percentages of convictions were as follows : —

	Death Penalty	Imprison-ment with hard labour	Imprison-ment	Fines
1882 - -	0.03	4.1	69.1	25.3
1892 - -	0.01	2.8	62.4	32.6
1902 - -	0.01	2.0	52.8	42.6
1912 - -	0.01	1.3	44.7	51.4
1925 - -	0.02	1.4	33.9	63.6

The numbers of cases of imprisonment have fallen from the three-fourths which it was originally, to close on a third. The advance made by imprisonment during the war and in the years immediately following the war, broke down in 1924 owing to the interference of the legislator. To-day (1932) the fine is the chief means of punishment in our penal code, which is all the more reason to pay increased attention to its effects and psychology. For the fine carries with it an unsolved problem, which endangers its employment, the question of not being able to enforce payment. The place of the fine is taken, according as it is a question of a crime, offence or infringement, by prison or custody. Apart from the maximum limit of a year for imprisonment in the two types of prison, and six weeks for custody, complete liberty is given to the Court in measuring the transmuted punishment. Thus the Court considers, corresponding to the law, imprisonment unsuitable. It inflicts a fine. If payment cannot be enforced, then there follows a transmutation into the form of punishment which the law either has not indicated at all or considers not to answer the purpose.

One could say with the English criminal statistics that the mere idea of such a sanction makes many people pay. " If this sanction did not exist, thousands would not pay their fines and thousands would not heed the law at all."

It is true that the English Criminal Justice Administration Act, 1914, does not allow the Courts to transmute the fine without further ceremony into imprisonment and that the German law (§ 29 Abs. 6) empowers the Court, if it wishes (' so kann das Gericht ') in cases of nonpayment for which the person is not to blame, not to proceed with the execution of the substitute punishment. All the same in 1928 13,260 people were imprisoned in England because they had not paid their fines, which is a tremendous advance when one considers that the figure in 1899 was 83,855 and a serious symptom against it, if we consider matters from another aspect. The complete discontinuance of the infliction of a substitute punishment, which the German law allows, is a highly imperfect and unsatisfying solution, but it at least takes into consideration the fact that the prisoner is subjected to extremely noxious influences from which he cannot get away. On the other hand, by serving a term of imprisonment the law's authority is preserved, only that which was formerly called wisdom of punishment (strafweisheit) is downright disregarded.

A punishment which is pronounced must be carried out or only for quite definite reasons temporarily suspended. The fine must be replaced by the computation according to ratios of value of the working-power. In any case this power of working must be taxed. The sentence primarily and on principle concerns a fixed amount of work production. In order to be able to realize this production, the convicted person must be given an opportunity to work and that in the simplest form of a productive employment which can be utilized by the State or the municipalities. Instead of transmuting the sentence into work, it can be transmuted into money, payment in instalments, or on account, and deductions in the case of those who have fixed salaries or those who have a claim on the State. Only if we go back to the power of working which the majority of people possess, will the idea of nonpayment disappear, will a mild form of punishment cease to be transmuted into a severe one, which is indeed only supposed to enforce payment and, if it does not work, only causes the State expense; and there will finally disappear from the world the unbearable fact (possible in Germany) that a fine is first inflicted, then because it is not paid, transmuted into imprisonment and then the imprisonment in its turn is not carried out because the convicted, with the best will in the world, was unable to pay.

In many cases it will be impossible to avoid returning to a form of confinement. But this detention is only to force out and control the work done. The prison, by remaining in which the convicted person pays the fine, is something quite different. Wherever it is possible, the amount of work imposed is to be procured by work done at large.

I have already spoken about the improved organization of compensation for damage in modern criminal procedure. The compensation for damage should accord the injured party that discharge of feeling which modern forms of criminal procedure only imperfectly vouchsafe him. Here the injured party should experience the State's care, which he otherwise always enviously sees given to the perpetrator. In the careful manipulation of reparation I see the one and only effective and calming treatment of the instinct of retaliation, which otherwise continually exercises a complicating and destructive interference on a calm policy of punishment.

To divest the fine of its character of purely fiscal receipt would lead to a more economical and considered administration. Still better than the proposal in Ferri's Bill, that the public prosecutor should be obliged to move the question of compensation for damage, is the regulation proposed in the Czecho-Slovakian Bill of 1926. Here the fine itself shall be used in payment of the damage done, if it has not been possible to carry through the claim for compensation from another quarter. Here, too, what remains over from the fines is to be used to set up a fund to make easier the care of discharged prisoners and of the families of prisoners undergoing a sentence. In special cases the Minister of Justice can also vouch-safe assistance from this fund to injured parties who have suffered an especially grievous injury.

As a punishment for smaller delicts, the perpetrator shall hand over a part of this working power, in one form or another, to the State, either in *natura*, or changed into terms of money. The way must be opened for delivery in kind; the task will not in every case be immediately demanded should this payment in kind be economically irrational; that is to say, it will be demanded from the peasant where possible in winter. The contribution of work or money will not have to be a source of purely fiscal income, but must benefit the injured party or serve certain purposes of the aid which is given before or after the execution of punishment. In practice this punishment will be chiefly a fine. It must never be transmuted into imprisonment as such. Only in those cases in which the work at large offered has not been carried out, can the State not renounce the compulsory delivery of a certain quantum of work. But here the confinement will not be an end in itself, but the organized frame for the compulsory production of the work.

8. DEROGATORY PUNISHMENTS

We can number deprivation of the right to burial and effacement from memory, measures of the praxis of penal law which we come across most in Roman law, among the derogatory punishments; only we must make it quite clear to ourselves that traditional rights which do not come within the modern conception of honour are here called in question. Here it is a question of forms of attack on the metaphysical existence of man, of destructive processes of the most energetic kind, which depend on the imagined and hoped-for scope of human punishments.

Refusal of burial was a secondary punishment, inflicted in conjunction with execution by the axe, crucifixion, execution at national festivals, and above all execution in prison. In cases of drowning and burning, the regular form of burial of itself did not take place. With execution in prison the executioner dragged the corpse with a hook on to the Gemonian steps, and then with the same hook through the streets and threw it into the river. A military guard was provided during the carrying out of this measure. One of the secondary results of banishment which aggravated the punishment was that of burial in the place of banishment.

Penal law also attacked the mourning of the deceased and any memorial service for the condemned. Thus Domitian had Salvius Coccejanus executed because he celebrated the birthday of Otho, his paternal uncle. On

226

the other hand, Nero's grave was for a long time deco-
rated with spring and summer flowers.

Finally, the condemned person's picture was pro-
scribed, his name erased, his statues overthrown, sometimes his house was razed and his name, which his own
family was no longer allowed to bear, was ' laid waste.'
We again come across this pursuit right into the last
hiding-places of the physical and metaphysical existence
among civilized peoples in other continents.

All these methods of punishing the dead remain incomprehensible unless we go back to the old belief of an
evil-bringing, restless haunting on the part of the dead.
The dead person returns, but one can bar his way back
by obliterating the tracks; one can make him lose his
way. The suicide is dragged through a hole under the
threshold. As soon as a corpse is outside the house,
every window and door is shut behind it, so that the dead
man loses the desire to go back. Water was poured
behind the dead person who is carried out of the house;
water forms the boundary between life and death, it
disenchants or scares away the spirits. In between come
other and later groups of ideas: he who hinders the care
or worship of the dead, lamentation for the dead, the
wake, the burial, or alms for the dead, interfere with
the darkened further existence of the dead. As Erwin
Rhode has said: " The souls are dependent on the
worship of those members of their family who are still
alive; their fate is decided according to this worship."
Praise, glory and remembrance make the dead person
powerful, and neglect powerless. Perhaps the devastation (' wüstung ') goes back to those far times when
the dead person was still buried inside the house where
he was worshipped. Thus it was not only the place to
which the demon would return that was destroyed and

barred, but also the place where prayers, offerings and loyal remembrance looked after the soul's welfare.

The original religious purpose of the devastation gradually changed and began to have the effect of punishment directed against property. It persisted in this form particularly long among the Friesians and was there transformed into quite an independent kind of punishment which was inflicted in addition to compensation and peace money. Devastation in cases of rape goes back to the earliest times. Friesian küren (Law books) in the eleventh century ordered to be razed, both the place where the crime was committed and all the houses into which the perpetrator had flown. A third conception regards the house like an animal, as a living creature which did not go to the help of the woman in her distress and therefore must be punished. " The village building whose walls and locks prevented the woman's escape and favoured such a sin, shall be destroyed because of this outrage. It must lie there desolate and broken up." This personification of beasts and things is surely the last effort at making a religious act of complete effacement of existence, which was born of fear, comprehensible to oneself and others. The raper's evil spirit has penetrated into every living creature which witnessed the infamous deed, into the walls and beams of the houses, and can only be banished by their destruction and dispersal. If later animals and house were regarded as abettors, it was then a question of a rational explanation of occurrences whose origin was no longer comprehensible.

Deprival of the right to burial was for those who believed in another world fundamentally a further ' death ' penalty. Loss of civic rights, loss of the right to make a will, which according to Mommsen was first

used as a general punishment during the persecution of
the Christians in the third century and was immediately
used against the conquered heathens by the Christianized
State, was a property punishment in the veiled form of
declaring a person incompetent to make a will, which
was joined by still further restriction of rights. Exclusion from candidature for office and prohibition of public
or private activity were securative measures which
accompanied the actual penal punishment.

The German law has developed real derogatory punishments in great variety—disavowal, apology, insulting
dress, a sword or halter round the neck, rods or besom
in the hand, carrying a saddle or a stone, being har-
nessed to the plough, riding an ass, unroofing, tar-and-
feathering, being pilloried and ducked, and other
methods which affected one's honour. But if we look
closer, we see severer means of punishing, means which
once affected body and life; for most of the derogatory
punishments are the rudiments of beheadal, hanging,
stoning, drowning, laying waste and scourging. That
they are derived from capital punishments in inferred by
the nakedness, which was originally requisite, or by the
mitigated forms of complete denudation, going barefoot
and wearing a hair shirt. In the true derogatory punishment of riding an ass which was prescribed for women
who fought or adulteresses, a much older origin is indicated by the fact that they rode backwards, the pelting
with bad eggs (relic of stoning?) and the accompanying
blowing of bugles. The harnessing to the plough also
reminds one of the manifold symbolism of the plough.
Drilling a furrow with a plough is a very old feature in
the paying of homage to a new master. In the punishment the place of the draught animal, mostly oxen, is
taken by the person of the erring man. Here the blowing

of bugles occurs again. The instrument which tears the surface of the ground, had a clear positive or negative affinity to the powers of the evil one.

Even the old German law had degrading punishments which, it is true, were regarded as defaming, but which gave an effect of security, like prohibition of carrying weapons, to which homicide and corporal injury gave rise. This was sometimes accompanied by a very energetic measure putting the inns out of bounds. The modern law's derogatory punishments are chiefly disguised, secondary property punishments; but at the same time there are a few measures affecting one's self-respect, permanent loss of public office, titles, orders or badges of honour.

The deprivation of civic rights is often annihilating as a property punishment, so destructive that the re-establishment of a civic existence becomes a problem. As a securative measure police guard is without effect; the restrictions imposed are assured by a slight threat of punishment. Inopportune imposition of the restriction frequently accelerates the relapse of the morally ' derailed.' As long as people lived in small towns or villages, everybody knew everybody else and depended on them and their estimation of his worth, and, further, as long as the sentence was surrounded with the halo of absolute justice certain derogatory punishments could exercise a social and regulating function. I remember that when I was in the army an old man was degraded to the second class for a small offence and went about the stable lines with only *one* cockade. At first a derogatory punishment made a great impression on the recruit, but then by constant association he became completely unconscious of it. Thus one can well understand it when purely derogatory punishments disappear more and more from the newer (or better said from the modern) penal codes. It persists in public opinion in the defamation of a previous conviction. Here its arbitrary, unfavourable effects are clearly evident.

The loss of fitness to bear office, of the right to vote, will remain as secondary punishments; only care must be taken that these secondary punishments are not debased to political weapons. So, according to the German Bill (1927), a person may be deprived of the right to hold office or to vote for the least hint of treasonable action, incitement to high treason or the preparation of high treason, without any consideration of the kind and extent of the punishment. Very inaptly, the preamble says, a person who is ' the enemy of every community ' must be eliminated from having an influence on the fate of the country. A perpetrator in whom the law itself presumes the possibility of respectable motives, must not be allowed to be separated from legal or political activity by means of penal law, even when this activity is dangerous or troublesome to the group in power. Penal law's intrinsically convincing and cogent power depends on the fact that it serves the permanent aims of the State and keeps as far away as possible from the fluctuating gamble of the struggle for power and the dispute as to forms of State.

CHAPTER V

THE DEVELOPMENT AND FUTURE OF
PUNISHMENT

The magical and religious foundations which we have excavated from under the visible walls of punishment do not only give an explanation of the form and contents of many means of punishment, but they, above all, help us to understand the tremendous tenacity with which capital, corporal and many derogatory punishments defend themselves in our emotional life against any rationalization. If, when a man is executed or flayed, it is not that human beings wish to attain a certain object in regard to the person who has been killed or flayed (and had to discontinue the treatment, in as far as the desired object is unobtainable), but that magical powers and divine beings intervene, then our incomplete experience and very earthly knowledge must abdicate.

The strategic positions of the mythical inside penal thought are so strong because up till now the fight against crime was waged without success and seemed to have as little chance as it would against natural catastrophes like earthquakes, volcanic eruptions and pandemias. They will be weakened if scientific research brings more clarity into our methods of punishment and the rows of figures in the statistics of crime, rightly selected, are thinned out. A ray of hope for penal law comes from the development of psychiatry; after that medicine had already wrenched itself away from its magical encirclement, psychiatry in the twentieth cen-

232

tury has become a completely secularized science and from this moment has begun to wrest a causal therapy from causal knowledge and gain successes step by step.

The road of progress in penal law is curiously zigzag. The need for punishment surges up in strange rhythms, sinks and suddenly returns in new disguises of a return to mysticism. For this reason it seems to me that it is not quite conclusive to appeal, as the newer Bills love to do, to the nation's feeling for what is right. Magical and religious memories are embedded in the masses and just there are the most deeply rooted. The psyche of women and the shrivelled up, timorous emotions of elderly people are inclined towards them. As the civilized States of Europe have a superfluity of women and the elder strata in the population grow up, the amystic criminal jurist has a difficult struggle. The forces which bear superstition and which call retrogression, return of the perfect antiquity and the beautiful past, gnaw at the dyke which science of the last fifty years has painfully built up. The advance of the metaphysical element in so physical an affair as the treatment of people must with a wave of the hand put to one side the, for us, decisive question of the effectiveness of punishment. The criterion of success or failure is not the experience of the law nor the notes of criminal statistics. The effectiveness of punishment, to which our most secret feelings ascribe magical or religious ends, the parrying of magic, evil powers or the propitiation of an angry deity, cannot be checked in a statistical department. Like general prevention and the deterrence of the masses, it lies outside the circle of our experience. Here the counter question is put, like a poisonous philtre, before us: what would have happened if we had not executed or flayed? Still more crime, failure of crops, inundation, pestilence, lost wars, all the evil which the gods send the nations in order to whip with scorpions those disobedient to their commandment. This conception counters our demonstration of the ineffectiveness of many means of punishment, with the assertion of an effectiveness which avoids being tested by man. In unlucky ages people listen to these arguments, for necessity teaches us not only to pray, but to believe, and faith gives quicker comfort than the slow progress of science is able to do.

But if we only stick to practical knowledge, the long history of criminal law, an endless history of errors and sometimes even of collective insanity, has shown one thing. Punishment affects the criminal, but it also affects the State. In the slow process of psychic refinement, the State, as model, plays a part which it has failed to recognize. Thus every punishment must be tested as to its dual effect. How does it affect the person condemned; and how does the act of punishing affect the receptive psyche of the other people into whose imagination it falls in some direct or indirect way? Before the punishment in its adaptation by higher brain centres takes on the emotional value of a deterrent, it passes through parts of the central nervous system, in which it is deposited as a colourless, devalued impression. If these deposits collect in large numbers, the person is unable to get away from the suggestion of this store of positive observations; the repeated perception of an act of violence, projected into the brain, develops motorial tendencies; familiarity with it destroys the deterrent vibration of synchronised emotionality, and what remains is a conception of the world, to whose components the act of punishing belongs, not as a punishment, but as an act, ordered and executed by the State itself, to which one has got used and which is directed against life or bodily integrity.

The State, as is shown by the history of the Roman emperors, finally perishes in this competition in brutalizing. For mass employment of brutal means of punishment consumes the limited powers of the State's authority; the final introduction of mild methods is exhaustion. In order to hide its defeat, there is associated with this weakness the readiness to accept new knowledge which has long been made known.

The effect of punishment results from a fixed relation between means of punishment and sensitivity to punishment. We take good care of the population's moral state if we increase its sensitivity to punishment and thus attain the same or a greater effect with slighter interference. But if with our punishment we put excessive demands on its sensitivity to punishment, it suffers and becomes callous. Punishment is the easiest form of settling a dispute or disposing of a difficulty, indeed, it is often only a settlement in appearance, because new problems follow on the heels of the execution which follows the quick sentence. That the law, judgment and punishment are the first to make a person criminal and to thrust him deeper and deeper into crime, is no rare occurrence.

Conscious economy with punishment means the refining of sensitivity to pain and thus an increase in the effect of punishment. I do not need to add that a criminologically just treatment must in many cases be directed against the crimogenous surroundings; that prevention belongs to the economy of punishment and that the personal and social wound of punishment should be closed by a careful after-treatment which re-enrolls the discharged prisoner in a family or social group and, above all, gives him work.

PUNISHMENT

Crime is *attack* on someone else's legal right. It is true that very many passive personalities, too, commit delicts, but all these types are moved, however inert they themselves are, by the impulse of another's stronger will or an oppressive state of conflict which supplements their crippled will. If we leave out of consideration the moribund capital and corporal punishment and the new method of sterilization which is coming into fashion, and if we further reserve for the less serious cases the punishment of exacting a tribute of working power (substitute punishment, a fine), then internment remains the chief means in the struggle against crime.

All the new methods of treatment: the curing of the insane cases, the reform of youths and certain types of grown-ups, the detention of the mentally inferior, invalids or active habitual criminals, need the frame of a mechanical seclusion from the outside world. Considerations of therapy and relevant psychiatric treatment demand custody in an institution, in addition to the securing of the sick person himself and of the public against him. In the case of youthful criminals and reformable adults that pause which permits of a gradual ' putting in plaster ' of will and feelings, and of a building up of desire for work and moral connexions is not possible without a lengthy detention. In the case of the habitual criminal and approximate types, we must confess our therapeutic helplessness; but we do not because of that forgo the protection of society. We will keep the chronic criminal secured in custody, without unnecessary infliction of pain but also without any dangerous sentimentality, until life has lost its danger for him and he his for it. This group will lose more and more of its opaqueness and intractability as our knowledge increases. If in the future criminals are divided

236

into subjects for medical and educative treatment, there will only be left a relatively small remnant which I would prefer to see deported. Against the utility of keeping them secluded in custody must be put a number of noxious factors, the massing together, which cannot be obviated for financial and technical reasons; the wearing away of the sense of honour, which is a well-known malady of confinement: the taking root of new, anti-social conceptions and ideas of society, which every prison brings about. Custody is further connected with corporal injury, with psychic devastation or over-excitement of emotionality, with a one-sided intellectual saturation, which frequently only reach as far as the technique of crime, and, finally, with a far-reaching reduction in suitability, for the world with its numerous conflicts and complications, is replaced by a relation between warders and prisoners, built up here on force, there on deceit. Here the warder is often only in semblance the superior, and through convenience becomes the prisoner of the prisoner. Such an artificial atmosphere reigns nowhere in real life, it deceives the prisoner as to the intelligence and the superiority of the people with whom he has hourly to do when he is free again.

For all these reasons the closed institution must be confined to the cases for whom permanent enclosure is absolutely requisite. I have demanded for part of the prisoners the open or semi-open institution. The efforts of America in this not only psychologically but also economically important question are exemplary.

The abstract classifications which we have just mentioned and associated with various methods of treatment, are provisional abstractions from living criminal material. More difficult than this scientific aggrupation is the practical task of rightly sorting out the inflowing material of prisoners and apportioning them to the appropriate institutions. The summary sifting undertaken by the penal code which clings to the facts of the case, is most disturbing; although the facts of cases are necessary for reasons of legal security and therefore unconditionally to be preserved, they are not opposed to a psychological appreciation. As it is one thing to establish the facts of a certain case, and another to regulate the treatment of a person, the future criminal Courts will be split up. Courts of Deeds will decide the question as to whether an individual has committed a certain punishable action. The convicted person will then be put into a large distributive institution where he will be psychiatrically, sociologically, and in the light of the psychology of work, carefully examined. The proposal of allotment with all its documents and proof comes before the Court of Treatment which allots him to a certain type of treatment. Over the Court of Deeds is the Court of Revision and there could be a Professional Court. The Court of Treatment of which a psychiater and a criminologist will be permanent members, along with the professional judge and chairman, examines at regular intervals, and also at any time at the instance of the superintendent of the institution, its decisions and alters the mode of treatment, shortens or lengthens the period of internment.

The more we remove the character of pure institution life from internment itself, the juster will our judgment of the criminal be. Good conduct cannot suffice for provisional release, for in free life good conduct at which the passive, the clever or the old hand most easily succeed, is not sufficient. While they are still in the institution, we must look round for more difficult series of reactions, for examples of real life, its incessant

238

struggles, temptations, decisions to be made, emotional crises and claims on the will. What is decisive in real life is not good conduct, but right conduct in the struggle for bread, wife, a roof over one's head and a job to do; all of which are reactions about which the prisoner never has to bother his head.

Every form of internment will be a punishment, even though it is no longer executed as capital or derogatory punishment. The ending of the internment will be earned with greater difficulty and more honourably, than it is with the retaliation which the law measures out exactly into terms of punishment and with which public opinion dogs the punished long after the law has finished with him.

It was the gods who formerly founded royal houses; gods descended to the wives of men, stood at the elbow of the great law-givers and advised them, and stood watchfully beside the judge at the ordeal. All that disappeared; only punishment still sinks its roots deep down into the remotest past. Like everything beneficial which was created in mystic darkness, like fire, we must pull punishment down from heaven on to earth. As long as punishment was recognizable by all as man's handiwork, fear and obscure superstition could advise the helpless multitude to overcome the danger by blindly hitting out.

Only the scientific consideration of the criminal will gradually, as in a purifying flame, anneal the dross of the past from the fear-ridden picture of the criminal. Perhaps we will do with these remains what they did in 1459 with the witch from Ursenerthal, whose sentence Osenbrüggen quotes: " Finally collect all the ashes together and strew them in the Reuss, so that no further damage may come from them."

INDEX

241

249

PATTERSON SMITH REPRINT SERIES IN
CRIMINOLOGY, LAW ENFORCEMENT, AND SOCIAL PROBLEMS

* new material added   † new edition, revised or enlarged

PATTERSON SMITH REPRINT SERIES IN
CRIMINOLOGY, LAW ENFORCEMENT, AND SOCIAL PROBLEMS

* new material added   † new edition, revised or enlarged